STRAIGHT TALK ABOUT THE FUTURE OF HUMANITY

STRAIGHT TALK ABOUT THE FUTURE OF HUMANITY

Will our intelligence save us or destroy us?

John Woolschlager Ph.D.

Book Layout © 2017 BookDesignTemplates.com

Straight Talk About the Future of Humanity/John Woolschlager Ph.D. -- 1st ed.
ISBN 979-8-8841-3368-6

*This book is dedicated to all who live today
and to those who may live in the future.*

Table of Contents

Acknowledgements...ix

Preface: Meet Dr. W. xi

THE END IS NEAR…AN INTRODUCTION 1

Read the warning label...3

Age of the "intelligent" animal 7

Apocalyptic dreams...15

We told you so 19

You can't handle the truth! 23

APOCALYPTIC BUFFET…FUTURE RISKS TO HUMANITY
....27

Risky business...29

Eight billion and counting…....................................32

Out of Africa 38

Eating a hole in the Earth 41

Don't waste my energy 45

Hunger games 49

Drop that deep-fried butter stick!..........................54

One word: plastics...58

A hot topic..62

Dr. Strangelove's doomsday machine 68

Oops, I just made COVID-666 74

Stop killer robots!.......................................80

But wait, there's more… 87

Natural apocalyptic alternatives.......................................91

The sum of all fears.......................................94

THE MANY EXCUSES WHY WE ARE NOT MAKING PROGRESS 103

Life is good 105

Twenty-nine dragons to slay 107

Alt facts and uncritical thinking.......................................110

Death by 1000 distractions.......................................114

House of cards.......................................117

The church of technology 121

IDEALISTIC PLANS AND REAL PROGRESS.......................................125

Plan Z 127

Sustainability and other dirty words 130

Let's do it like they do it in Finland.......................................135

Dr. W.'s dire forecast for humanity 139

The alternative happy ending.......................................144

Notes 155

Acknowledgements

I would like to acknowledge the many educators, advisors, colleagues, and friends who helped me gain the knowledge, skills, perspective, and inspiration to write this book. There are too many of you to name here, but you know who you are.

I want to name those who specifically helped me with this book project. I want to thank Deborah Murrell who copy-edited this book with skill, professionalism, and precision. A special thanks Tara Norton, Frank Händle, Brian Carter, and Annabelle Nyren for reading my manuscript and giving me valuable feedback that greatly improved this work.

Preface: Meet Dr. W.

"I'm as mad as hell and I'm not going to take this anymore!"
— Howard Beale, a fictional character from the film *Network* brilliantly played by Peter Finch.

Like Howard Beale, I'm mad as hell, so much so that you could call me *The Angry Environmentalist*. How did this happen to such a nice guy? I have worked hard for over thirty years to help protect the environment and prevent humanity from suffering a self-induced catastrophe. But as I and many other eco-warriors have toiled, we have lost more ground than we have gained. I've grown tired of watching humanity slowly spiral down the toilet of destiny. The maddening thing is that we have the knowledge and ability to solve all the problems we keep creating. But we are not getting it done. This book is the fruit of my anger and concern—my swan song endeavor to make a difference.

My name is John Woolschlager. My students called me "Dr. W." because my 12-letter last name often got butchered. Even when I presented a PowerPoint slide explaining that it is pronounced "Wool" like what covers a sheep and ends in "lager" like a type of beer, many of my students still didn't get it. So, I settled for being called Dr. W. and I'm sticking with it. I have a Ph.D. in Environmental Engineering and have worked at various universities in the US. I've held several impressive-sounding positions, including one that called me an "Eminent Scholar Professor," which I often joked as being the "Impotent Scholar Professor."

I was not born anywhere near the ivory tower that I would later climb. I am from Oak Cliff, Texas, an inner-city neighborhood in the shadow of downtown Dallas. Back then it was a racially diverse, mostly working-class part of town. I was far from being born with a silver spoon in my mouth. In fact, I was more likely to have a wooden spoon whacked across my head or my backside.

I was not a good student. I was generally bored in school. I spent most of my time sleeping with my head on a desk or in the principal's office getting lectured or paddled. I stumbled through school, eventually graduating in the third quarter of my high school class. Career advisors urged me to consider learning a trade and getting straight to work. I had worked several summers for my grandfather's remodeling company, so it seemed my destiny was to march forward through life with a hammer in hand. But many of the girls I liked left for college, so I decided to follow them and give higher education a try. After two years, I met a girl, dropped out of college, got married, and started working as an engineering technician for a military aircraft company. It was not the worst job I could have landed, but it was not what I really wanted. Soon I was bored again, this time sleeping in the bathroom stall or standing in my boss's office trying to justify my existence.

After years of doing tedious work just to earn a paycheck, I saved enough money to return to college and finish my degree. This time I was highly motivated—I worked hard and got straight A's. My good grades, stupid ambition, and a little luck got me a full-ride scholarship at Northwestern University to pursue my Ph.D. In 2000 I finally finished my degree. My first academic job was in Florida—in the sunshine and near the beach. Life was good. Although I often criticize the United States, I must admit it truly is the land of opportunity. There are few places on this Earth where someone with my start could end up becoming a university professor. The US is a great place to work but I would not want to live there, and I don't.

I am not telling you my life story because I think it is so interesting. Many have lived more exciting and accomplished lives. I am telling it to you because it's important to know that for a big part of my life I was just an average Joe. I know what is like to grow up in a tough neighborhood with few resources. I have worked mind-numbing jobs just to pay the bills. I have been so preoccupied with overcoming the daily hurdles of life that I did not give much thought to how I impacted the planet or our future. But I have also been lucky enough to have worked as a university professor with time to research, reflect on, and teach others about our environment and living sustainably. This experience allows me to better understand how the average Joe and Jane live and what it might take to get them on board with protecting our planet and our future.

My success in the academic world allowed me to retire early and move to Spain in 2019. My motivation was to live a simpler and more sustainable life and have the time to write about a topic I truly cared about—the future of humanity. It turned out to be a great time to start writing on that topic. Trump was in office talking about having a "bigger button" to launch his nukes and the COVID pandemic had us locked up watching news reports showing ERs full of dying patients on respirators. It seemed the end may be nearer than I originally thought. I wrote several versions of this book. The first focused on the Trump administration's devastating impact on the environment. But that idea evaporated when Biden won the 2020 election. The second version of my book focused on the future of humanity, citing the many risks we are creating, pointing out that we are doing too little, and presenting a plan to save us from ourselves. I gave the first draft to my partner to read. In about five minutes I found her snoozing with the book draft sprawled on the floor beside her. That was not a good sign.

There are many reasons why this draft of my book did not work. It's a formula that has been done and redone many times over the past 50 years—warning us that we are destroying our planet and our future, lamenting that we are doing too little, and creating idealistic plans to save humanity that will never be implemented. Many of these books take on an optimistic tone about the future—putting a smiley face on the topic. But mine did not. When you read the unfiltered truth about our future it makes you want to curl up in a fetal position and go to sleep. That is exactly what my partner did.

I was ready to throw out the manuscript, go to the nearest café, order a wine or three, and enjoy the Spanish sunshine. During a depressive stupor that followed, I started binge-watching YouTube clips of some of my favorite comedians: Bill Maher, George Carlin, and Ricky Gervais. After hours of bathing myself in socially critical caustic comedy, I suddenly rose to my feet, like Archimedes rose out of his bathtub, and had a *eureka!* moment. I realized that my true inner voice is highly critical with a dose of caustic humor. I immediately set off to rewrite my book using my true voice. The words poured onto the page like one of those pineapple express storms that have been ravaging California lately. The result was surprising and a little scary. It was in a different universe from my academic writings. I sent my first draft out to a few readers to make sure it was not the ramblings of a lunatic. The reader comments were positive, and they helped me tone things down a bit. After a few more rounds of editing, I decided to leap off the cliff and publish this book. So, if you love it, you can call me "A genius who brings a fresh voice to important issues." If you hate it, blame Bill, George, and Ricky for inspiring me to unleash my inner Texan.

Of course, that's a joke. I own my writing and I am proud of it. Haters, don't waste your time attacking me on social media—I will be too busy sipping a Tinto de Verano in the Spanish sunshine to read your drivel.

Happy reading!
Dr. W.
March 25, 2024
Xàbia Spain

THE END IS NEAR…AN INTRODUCTION

"Can you be more specific?"

Read the warning label

I am about to tell you the unfiltered truth about our future. I will be critical and forceful. Why am I doing this? Because for too long we have talked too much and done too little about how we impact our planet and our future. Talk, talk, talk…we love to proclaim our ideas about saving the Earth and humanity. There are so many books, films, TV programs, articles, and speeches on this topic that even ChatGPT may have trouble assimilating it all. I admit that we have made some progress, but if you look at how billions of us live, we are rapidly heading in the wrong direction. We have more people, consume more stuff, create more pollution, and have destroyed more natural habitats than ever before. We still have enough nukes to kill us all and we are creating new technologies that are more dangerous. Here's the rub—we need billions on board with living more sustainably to lower our risk for a catastrophe. A few thousand vegans living in eco villages will not save us.

How do I know our future is at risk? No, I am not a psychic. No, I did not read it on Facebook, Instagram, TikTok, or X. No, I did not pull it out of my hat or any other place. I am a professor who has studied, taught, and reflected on this topic for 30 years. And it's not just my opinion. Publications by leading experts have been clearly saying this since the 60s. Now the threat level is higher than ever. The message is not trickling down from the ivory tower because academic writing tends to be dull and obscure. The method to my madness is to decode academic jargon into a clear language that is easy to comprehend while adding a little humor to make this gloomy topic more palatable.

This book is a collection of short musings about the future of humanity that stand on their own. These can be read easily in small chunks of time, making this a great book to leave near the toilet—saving humanity one flush at a time. These musings are organized in sections so they can be stitched together to convey a larger message. Part one contains a few introductory topics on the possible demise of humanity; Part two describes the major risks we are creating that threaten our future; Part three explains the many excuses we use for not making progress; and Part four summarizes past and current ideas that could save humanity and points out what works and what doesn't.

Although humanity faces many risks, our demise is not certain. We humans have done amazing feats overcoming countless challenges. We can reduce the risks that threaten our future. We generally know what we should do, know how to do it, and have the resources to do it. What we lack is the social and political will to get it done. For example, we can eliminate the threat of nuclear weapons by simply disarming existing weapons and tightly controlling the technologies and materials needed to build new ones. But doing this requires high levels of international cooperation, trust, and verification. With ongoing threats of Putin going nuclear over Ukraine, progress on this issue is not likely anytime soon. But with a transformational shift in social and political attitudes, this and many other problems can be solved. I am not saying that would be easy nor do I see that happening any time soon. But I do believe that it is possible.

I hope that you can digest the contents of this book and what comes out the other end gives you a proper sense of urgency and a better understanding of what needs to be done to save ourselves from the risks we keep creating. We are at a tipping point that will determine our future. It's time to go big or go start building our survival shelters.[1]

One final word for the socially sensitive, telling the unfiltered truth about our future requires me to turn my filter off. I expect that some of my opinions and humor may be offensive. I don't intend to hurt anyone's feelings. I am purposely getting in the face of humanity to help save it. Think of it as a last-chance intervention. If I start filtering myself, this message will become watered down and ineffective, like mixed drinks at a cheap bar. You don't whisper "be careful" if someone you care about is about to stumble onto a busy motorway, you yell "watch out!" as you shove them back onto the sidewalk. Humanity needs to hear straight talk about our future and that is what I am delivering.

Age of the "intelligent" animal

"But man is a part of nature, and his war against nature is inevitably a war against himself."
— Rachel Carson, who published *Silent Spring* in 1962, a pivotal book that helped spark the environmental movement of the 60s and 70s.

We modern humans evolved to have bigger brains with superior intelligence that greatly distinguished us from the other human species that we originally shared the planet with. This was the beginning of a very interesting experiment. How would our new species use its superior intelligence? Would we use it to dominate and deplete the environment or protect and share it? How would we treat other humans and animals? Considering most mammals become extinct within about a million years, how long would our species survive? Would we use our intelligence to become the masters of our own destiny and survive for millions or even billions of years, or would we be overly successful, ravaging our environment, leading to our own demise within thousands of years? We know the answers to some of these questions, but how this experiment ends is yet to be determined.

Our self-proclaimed scientific name is *Homo sapiens*, which is Latin for "wise man." It fits our species well because our intelligence has given us the power to manipulate our environment far beyond any other species. Our impact is so great that we are starting to call this geologic time the Anthropocene—the Age of Man.[2] There is no place on Earth left untouched by our hands, no ecosystem unaltered, no virgin landscape that remains. This is bad news for the other creatures that share this planet with us, especially the many we are already wiping out. The intelligence that has given us such great power is also creating serious risks for our own species. Without a significant change in our direction, we may end up wiping ourselves out.

To understand how we got here, it's good to know a little about our family history. Around 2.5 million years ago, early humans were hunters and gatherers.[3] They used basic stone and bone tools for gathering nuts and vegetation and for hunting mostly small animals. Human populations were very low and had little impact on the planet. They were living in a Garden of Eden where all the resources they needed were supplied by nature.

About 300,000 years ago, we *Homo sapiens* arrived on the scene as the last member of the human family tree. For over 200,000 years we lived confined to mostly east Africa, not making much progress. You might say we were slow learners. About 55,000 years ago we overcame this limitation and started a major migration to the Middle East and later to Europe, Asia, and other continents. Like a deadly disease, where sapiens spread other species died off. The Neanderthals, the last major competing human species, were driven to extinction about 40,000 years ago. It is not known if we assimilated Neanderthals through interbreeding, outcompeted them for resources, or simply killed them. Since only a small percentage of our genetic code comes from Neanderthals, it is not likely much interbreeding took place.[4] It seems that we are more interested in breeding with Neanderthal types today than we were back then.

By around 15,000 years ago sapiens had spread to the Americas.[5] Where we lived many large mammals disappeared, such as the woolly mammoth and the American mastodon.[6] This marks the first time we had a significant impact on the planet. These great creatures will never walk the Earth again, along with all the other members of our human family. Our dubious success can be attributed to our superior intelligence and communication skills, allowing us to plan and implement goals across large groups.

We began farming and herding wild animals around 12,000 years ago[7]. Agriculture not only made our food supplies more reliable, but also allowed us to stay in one place, facilitating the establishment of stable communities that supported higher population growth. Of course, the land we cultivated for farming and ranching reduced the amount of natural habitat supporting other plants and animals. Our population around the start of agriculture was around 5 million,[8] so our impact to the global environment was still very limited.

The development of writing around 5,400 years ago allowed us to coordinate across even larger groups and pass knowledge to future generations, greatly increasing our collective intelligence.[9] About the same time, we saw the development of complex societies that dominated large territories in Mesopotamia, Ancient Egypt, and Ancient India. Our global population around this time is estimated to have been 14 million, the size of just one of today's large cities. Although gathering and processing materials for early civilizations certainly had local environmental impacts, the overall impact on the planet was still relatively small compared to today. The Earth still had vast areas of natural lands untouched by humans.

By the year 1 CE, our population had risen to between 170 and 400 million. Civilizations had become empires spread across vast lands. This was the time of the Roman Empire, the Mayan civilization, and the Han dynasty. Humans could travel great distances on roads or by sea. With increased population, development, and travel, our environmental impact was increasing, laying the foundation for much larger impacts to come.

About 500 years ago Gutenberg's printing press and the Scientific Revolution supported a knowledge explosion in Europe.[10] This laid the foundation for the Industrial Revolution, which not only changed business, jobs, and economics, but also significantly changed the basic structures of society, greatly magnifying our impact on the planet. From the late 1700s to the early 1800s, the Industrial Revolution started in Great Britain and quickly spread to continental Europe and the United States.[11] Farming work transitioned from being done by animals to using machines. Production of goods shifted from being handmade to being machine-made. New more efficient and compact steam engines fueled by coal powered the industrial and transportation systems of the time. Growth in manufacturing jobs skyrocketed in textiles, steel production, and making machine tools, supporting high economic and population growth in cities. Our population shot above one billion for the first time in 1804, beginning an explosive growth spurt that continues today.

The Industrial Revolution was the turning point enabling us to have a broad and substantial impact on the planet. High population growth and increased goods production along with higher per capita incomes led to higher consumption of natural resources and more pollution. Cities experienced air pollution events that made going outdoors intolerable.[12] Rivers became heavily polluted, impacting fish, wildlife, and drinking water supplies. Some rivers became so polluted that they could catch on fire due to the methane bubbling through anoxic waters.[13] Agriculture and urbanization rapidly expanded to support our explosive population growth, greatly reducing natural habitat, driving native animals into smaller spaces to survive. Flying over the US today it's easy to see the result—a continuous patchwork of farms between islands of urbanization. Most of the natural lands that remain are either too dry to farm or too costly to develop.

Now we are experiencing an Information Revolution.[14] If you are over 55, you may remember putting a floppy drive into an Apple II or IBM 5150 personal computer when they became popular in the late 1970s. If you are over forty, you may recall sending your first email when the World Wide Web went public in the 1990s. For younger readers, perhaps you remember when you first discovered the Google web search engine or when you posted personal information on Facebook or Myspace when they became popular in the early 2000s. These three components—wide access to computers, broad use of the Internet, and the collection and dissemination of data—led to the greatest expansion of information access in human history. Despite our increased access to knowledge, we continued to degrade our planet.

To put the pace of human development in perspective, imagine that we create a clock where 24 hours represents the 300,000 years of *Homo sapiens'* existence—hour 0 is 300,000 years ago and midnight represents the year 2024. On the clock, agriculture did not begin until eleven pm, the Industrial Revolution began about one minute and fourteen seconds before midnight, and the Information Revolution began thirteen seconds before midnight. And much has changed since then. When I was a teenager in 1977, I could not have imagined the world we live in today. The pace of change is expected to accelerate—a thought that is exciting and scary at the same time—like BASE jumping into the future.

Today, through technologies created by our intelligence, we live longer, healthier, and more comfortable lives. Technology is not just gadgets like computers, mobile phones, and those annoying drones buzzing overhead. Technology provides us with daily essentials such as food, water, energy, health care, and communications. Our comfortable climate-controlled homes are made possible by technology. Technology gives us instant access to a universe of knowledge through supercomputer telephones that can fit in our pockets and keep us occupied for endless hours. But some of these technologies are generating significant risks to our future. The 1938 discovery of atomic fission made available an abundant new energy source but also resulted in the creation of nuclear weapons with the potential to destroy all of us.[15] Now we are developing new technologies even more dangerous. It is not just these high-tech risks that threaten our future. The agricultural and industrial revolutions provided abundant food and wealth that supported explosive human population growth, resulting in greatly diminished natural resources, a severely damaged environment, and a rapidly changing climate.

The intelligence that has created abundant wealth and comfort is threatening our future. Will our intelligence save us or destroy us? Will we keep going down the same risky path? Or will we become a smarter species willing to do what it takes to protect our planet and secure our future? Of course, that depends on us, and that's what worries me.

Apocalyptic dreams

I looked when He opened the sixth seal, and behold, there was a great earthquake; and the sun became black as sackcloth of hair, and the moon became like blood. And the stars of heaven fell to the earth, as a fig tree drops its late figs when it is shaken by a mighty wind. Then the sky receded as a scroll when it is rolled up, and every mountain and island was moved out of its place.
— Revelations 6:12-14

Although I deeply care about the future of humanity, I must confess that I love apocalyptic movies. I have been thoroughly entertained by these films showing humanity destroying itself by various means. We have been nuked by an insane general who started a war with Russia because he believed "our precious bodily fluids were being impurified by the communists" in *Dr. Strangelove*. We have exposed ourselves to viruses that either kill us or turn us into zombies in *The 12 Monkeys* and *The Omega Man*. And we created artificial intelligence systems that quickly decided humans were a threat and sent a naked Arnold Schwarzenegger back from the future to kill us in *The Terminator*. These classic movies depict scary but fascinating visions of our future.

Apocalyptic stories are nothing new. Ever read *The Book of Revelation* in the Bible? It is a freaky story starring all kinds of strange creatures delivering a variety of vile pestilences to the unfaithful remains of humanity. The story features a lamb with seven horns and eyes; four scary horsemen delivering conflict, war, hunger, and death; and swarms of locusts with human faces with mouths full of lion's teeth. Earlier books in the Bible include numerous apocalyptic events that document the demise of millions killed by God, usually by some horrible means.[16] I guess they deserved it.

Why are we so fascinated with apocalyptic stories? Perhaps we believe that this is where humanity is heading. Psychologists call this the "Armageddon Complex" that creates much anxiety around events such as the Blood Moon.[17] Much of this is driven by fear created by religious superstitions that are part of every culture. These fears enter our subconscious and our dreams. Psychological data suggests that apocalyptic dreams are a widespread phenomenon, historically and cross-culturally.[18]

Another possible reason for our apocalyptic fascination is our craving for adventure—we get bored and need to be shaken up a bit to keep things fresh. Psychological research infers that humans need to be challenged to achieve optimum wellbeing.[19] This idea is reflected in films like *Pleasantville* and *The Matrix,* where perfect worlds led to unhappiness and disfunction. During breaks taken while writing this book, I would waste hours playing Minesweeper, a silly online game where you guess which squares have hidden mines. Why did I do this? Because I needed a mini adventure to get my blood pumping again, even if it was just looking for imaginary mines on my computer. Anyone who has played video games knows that the popular ones always involve some sort of danger—such as hand-to-hand combat, driving fast cars, or doing something naughty in *Second Life.* Hopefully we can find constructive ways to satisfy our sense of adventure that doesn't involve living through an apocalypse. Perhaps we can go on journeys in the metaverse as Arnold Schwarzenegger did in *Total Recall*.

The unfortunate truth is many believe that humanity is destined toward an apocalypse because of the abundant data showing that we are heading in that direction. I believe it. Many of my friends and colleagues believe it, but quickly switch the conversation to politics to lighten things up. My partner believes it, but she doesn't want to talk about it because it's too depressing. More importantly, leading experts have presented evidence supporting this idea for over 50 years. This is bad news unless you are a survivalist hiding in a basement quietly yearning for the battle of Armageddon to begin.

Regardless of the reason, the idea that humanity is heading toward an apocalypse seems to be embedded in our psyche. When our expectations lead to actions that become our reality, psychologists call it a *self-fulfilling prophecy*.[20] Humanity needs to get a new vision of our future fast before our apocalyptic dreams become our living nightmare.

We told you so

"One of the penalties of an ecological education is that one lives alone in a world of wounds."
— Aldo Leopold, considered the godfather of environmental ethics.

We have known for a long time that we are damaging the planet and putting our future in peril. Around 400 BCE, the Greek physician Hippocrates observed that some health problems were likely caused by environmental pollution.[21] The book *An Essay on the Principle of Population,* published in 1798 by Thomas Robert Malthus, warned of future difficulties because the population was doubling every 25 years and outpacing increases in food production, creating the fear of widespread famine. In the 1800s Henry David Thoreau wrote his seminal ecological treatise *Walden,* and George Perkins Marsh wrote *Man and Nature,* denouncing humanity's indiscriminate "warfare" upon the wilderness.

In the 1900s environmental ethics greatly evolved. In 1949 Aldo Leopold wrote in *A Sand County Almanac* "...a thing is right when it tends to preserve the integrity, stability, and beauty of the biotic community. It is wrong when it tends otherwise." Albert Einstein felt morally troubled by his contribution to the development of nuclear weapons and drafted an anti-nuclear manifesto in 1955 with British philosopher Bertrand Russell that was signed by ten Nobel Prize winners.[22]

In the 60s and 70s we experienced an environmental awakening. The 1962 publication of *Silent Spring* by Rachel Carson opened our eyes to the impact of chemical pesticides on birds. Guess what? Her predictions were spot on. According to a recent comprehensive study, nearly half of the world's bird species are now in decline and one in eight species (1,409 species total) are now threatened with extinction. Nearly three billion birds are estimated to have been lost since 1970 in North America and 600 million have been lost in the European Union.[23] As I hike through the Spanish wilderness I see or hear few birds. When I reflect on my youth, I recall seeing birds everywhere. There were blue jays, robins, cardinals, mockingbirds, and loads of sparrows hopping about the grass, sitting in trees, and harassing the cats. It's sad to see that silent spring has arrived.

Other landmark books published in the 60s and 70s expanded our awareness of environmental issues. *The Population Bomb* by Paul Ehrlich made us keenly aware of explosive population growth and the ramifications it has on the environment and our future. *Operating Manual for Spaceship Earth* by Buckminster Fuller made us aware of the resource limitations of our planet. In 1972 *Limits of Growth* included projections done by a group of top researchers that showed if population growth and resource consumption continued at the same pace, it would have devastating impacts on the environment, and humanity could eventually take a fall. A review of their predictions 50 years later shows that they are still holding true.

This environmental awakening fully crystallized on April 22, 1970, when 20 million people gathered to protest environmental destruction during the first Earth Day.[24] It remains the largest single-day protest in human history. The first Earth Day events took place in towns big and small across the US. Congress was adjourned to allow politicians to participate. Earth Day created a broad movement focused on protecting our planet. The next day these activists did not put away their protest signs and return to business as usual. They went after members of Congress with poor environmental records, eventually showing seven of them to the door. This got Congress' attention, resulting in the creation of the Environmental Protection Agency and the passing of numerous laws that cleaned up the air, water, and land, and protected natural resources and endangered species. A shining example of how to get stuff done that we should "recycle" today.

We all know what happened next. The 80s made a sharp turn away from the environment with a dominance of conservatism and support for free market economics, less regulation, and lower taxes for the wealthy. This was the decade of the yuppie, Reagan, and Thatcher. The 90s gave us the Internet, the mullet, rollerblades, and *The Wolf of Wall Street*. The 2000s kept us well distracted with 9/11 and the Gulf War, the proliferation of social media, and the 2008-2009 financial crisis. The 2000s also gave us a flood of new distracting technologies that dramatically changed the way we work, live, and find a restaurant. One bright spot was the 2006 release of *An Inconvenient Truth* by Al Gore that helped to catalyze concern about global warming.

For over 50 years we have been aware of the threats we are creating to the environment and our future. Since then, our population has more than doubled and we use more resources per person than ever before. Looking back, will we learn a valuable lesson from our mistakes and act? Or will we waste another five decades as the risk of our demise looms larger? Quoting John Connor in *Terminator 2*, "The future's not set. There's no fate but what we make for ourselves."[25]

You can't handle the truth!

*"Rather than love, than money, than fame,
give me truth."*
— Henry David Thoreau, *Walden*

It has come to my attention that it is frowned upon to be negative about the future of humanity. This seems especially true in university environments where I have worked. The idea is that too much negativity will make everyone want to give up. I have heard this idea echoed in campus presentations by well-known environmentalists. I have read it in environmental articles and books. I have seen this during my class lectures—students tend to curl up into fetal positions and want to go to sleep when I get too serious about environmental issues. Some of my friends seem to do the same. This makes me want to channel my inner Jack Nicholson and scream "You can't handle the truth!"[26] But I am afraid that would scare people even more.

The problem with this idea is that it prevents us from facing reality. It is essential that we fully understand the magnitude of future challenges so that we can properly gage our response to the level of the threat. If you are riding in a party bus with an on-board margarita machine, you probably don't want to be bothered about the road conditions. But if the bus is speeding toward a cliff where the bridge is out you will want to quickly steer the bus in a different direction. We are all on that party bus and it's time for us to drop the plastic cups and change our course.

Although we face serious threats, I am not an extreme environmentalist standing on the corner holding a sign saying, "The End is Near." Nor am I a Pollyanna technocrat telling you that we have a bright future ahead full of endless possibilities. The truth is somewhere in the middle of those extremes. We need to get serious about the risks that we are creating and take intelligent actions to reduce them. These are times for straight talk and game-changing action. Soft talk and half measures are no longer sufficient.

Heads up—there will be no participation trophies during an apocalypse. There will be the winners—the strong and ruthless people who will do anything to survive, and the rest of us will be what's for dinner. If you think that seems harsh, I suggest watching the post-apocalyptic movie *The Road*— hands down the most realistic representation of what humanity would look like if our social-technological systems broke down. The film is based on Cormac McCarthy's 2006 award-winning novel. It tells the story of a grueling journey of a father and his son over a period of several months across a harsh post-apocalyptic landscape. The father carries a gun loaded with two bullets, one for him and the other for his son, just in case they're caught by the roving gangs looking for fresh meat. McCarthy never reveals the cause of the apocalypse, which is very clever considering there are numerous threats that could bring us down. In the next section, I examine the major risks that threaten our downfall, hopefully helping us to take a different road in our future.

PART TWO

APOCALYPTIC BUFFET…FUTURE RISKS TO HUMANITY

"Don't be silly - the Sun won't burn itself out for another 5 billion years. Besides, the Earth will have been smashed to smithereens by asteroids long before that."

Risky business

"Risk is good. Not properly managing your risk is a dangerous leap."
— Evel Knievel, famous for his daring motorcycle jumps in the 60s and 70s.

Risk is part of everyday life. There is a significant risk involved in driving a car, walking downstairs, and even eating a piece of chicken. Risk is usually expressed as the chance of something bad happening over time. Over an average lifespan, the odds of dying from heart disease are 1 in 6 and dying from cancer are 1 in 7[1]. It may surprise you that the odds of dying from suicide or an opioid overdose are higher than the odds of dying in a car crash. Equally surprising is that the odds of dying from a fall are twice as high as the odds of dying from gun violence in the US. It seems that we need to ban the sale of AR-15s and extension ladders.

Humanity lives with risks on a global scale. The study of global risks is expanding rapidly, leading to the creation of research centers such as the Future of Humanity Institute at the University of Oxford. Researchers define an *existential risk* as one that threatens the premature extinction of humanity or eliminates the potential for desirable future development[2]. Note that an existential risk need not kill all of us. If a tragedy leaves just a few survivors in a state unable to rebuild any sort of desirable society, then it would qualify as an existential event. But there are serious disasters that do not rise to the existential level. To capture these events, I define a *global catastrophe* as an event that kills over 25% of the human population. I think that it is unwise to just focus on existential risks, because global catastrophes are much more likely to happen. Humans are like cockroaches—it will be very difficult to exterminate all of us.

The musings that follow examine various risks to humanity. Instead of presenting the high-risk topics first, I present them in the order in which they are more likely to affect our lives now, saving the high-tech futuristic risks until the end of the section. I start the section with several musings focused on our impact on the environment, followed by some on climate change and other risks.

Before continuing, I want you to do a fun little exercise. Make a list of what you think are the highest risks to our future. Feel free to list any apocalyptic ideas you fancy. Now, assign risk odds to each item on your list—the chances you think it will happen over the next century. For example, 1 in 10 odds work out to be a 10% chance; 1 in 100 odds equal 1%; 1 in 1,000 odds equal 0.1%; 1 in 10,000 odds equal 0.01%. You get the idea. As a point of reference, the odds of winning a Powerball jackpot are 1 in 292,201,338 or 0.00000034%. Hang on to your list to compare it to results revealed in the last muse in this section. Don't flip ahead, read the following musings in the order presented to truly savor this apocalyptic buffet of risks.

Eight billion and counting…

Source: Waitbutwhy.com[3]

On November 15, 2022, the United Nations published a feel-good story including the following quote:[4]

> *"This year's World Population Day falls during a milestone year, when we anticipate the birth of the Earth's eight billionth inhabitant. This is an occasion to celebrate our diversity, recognize our common humanity, and marvel at advancements in health that have extended lifespans and*

dramatically reduced maternal and child mortality rates..."

Passing the mark of the world having eight billion resource depleting and polluting souls should be a cause of concern, not for celebration. Our planet has limited resources that can only support so many of us. Among 65 studies estimating the maximum people the earth can support, more than half concluded that the Earth can only support eight billion or fewer of us.[5]

Human overpopulation is not a new issue. In the 1970s overpopulation became a popular topic in literature and film. One of my favorite post-apocalyptic films is *Soylent Green* released in 1973. The film is set in the year 2022 when the cumulative effects of overpopulation, pollution, and a climate catastrophe have caused severe worldwide shortages of food and other resources. Only the elite have access to natural food, fresh water, and secure homes that are fortified and guarded by private security. The poor live in squalor, haul water from communal spigots, and eat highly processed wafers; "Soylent Red," "Soylent Yellow," and the latest product, the far more flavorful and nutritious, "Soylent Green." Detective Robert Thorn, played by Charlton Heston, is tasked with investigating the murder of a wealthy and influential member of the Soylent Corporation board of directors. The investigation leads Thorn to the shocking discovery of what Soylent Green is really made from. If you don't know, I won't spoil the surprise—watch this outstanding film and find out for yourself. I will tell you that it's not vegan. Although we have passed 2022 without the vision of Soylent Green being realized, the film is a good representation of what might happen when we mix too many people with too few resources. The rich will be fine. The rest of us will eat Soylent Green if we are lucky.

How did we get into this mess? For most of our 300,000-year history, human populations were limited to 6-10 million people, less than the population of a single city today. The development of agriculture allowed humans to have more control over food supplies, supporting higher populations. The Industrial Revolution greatly increased productivity and created the infrastructure needed for humans to live and work in large cities, supporting explosive population growth that continues today. At the beginning of the Industrial Revolution the population reached 1 billion; 2 billion by 1920; 3 billion by 1960; 4 billion by 1974; 5 billion by 1987; 6 billion by 1999; 7 billion in 2011; and exceeded 8 billion in early 2023. Looking at this data as a chart, it looks like a rocket taking off into space. This growth is clearly not sustainable.

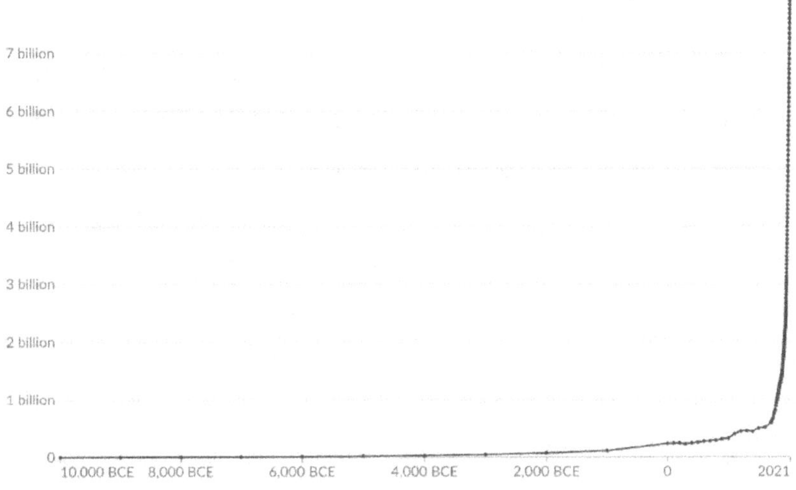

Population 10,000 BCE to 2021. Source: OurWorldinData.org.[6]

The good news is that population growth is expected to slow. As nations become more economically developed the population growth rate tends to diminish. The populations of 61 countries are expected to decrease by 2050, of which 26 will see a reduction of at least ten percent.[7] The United Nations projects the future population to reach 9.7 billion in 2050 and peak at 11.2 billion around 2100.[8] Will the Earth be able to support this number? I guess that we will find out. Allowing population growth to go unchecked puts more pressure on resources and the environment. Over time the planet will recover, but I am not sure how things will work out for us.

To pour acid on this wound, there are geniuses out there strongly promoting increasing our population. Matthew

Yglesias in his book *One Billion Americans: The Case for Thinking Bigger* argues that America is not over-crowded and could support one billion citizens. It makes the case that America has space for more people and that we need to increase our population to stay relevant in the future. To do so, it will need to be populated like China and India. Of course, we have space on Earth to crowd in more people, the question is do we have the physical and economic resources to support them.

Quiverfull is a Christian movement that sees large families as a blessing from God and encourages abstaining from all forms of birth control.[9] They quote Psalm 127:3-5 as their rallying cry to procreate:

> *"Lo, children are an heritage of the LORD: and the fruit of the womb is his reward. As arrows are in the hand of a mighty man; so are children of the youth. Happy is the man that hath his quiver full of them…"*

Similar ideas are promoted by other religious groups. This kind of nonsense is the population equivalent to not believing in climate change. Every person added to our planet increases risks to all of us, especially those living in less developed nations. Yes, there are reasonable arguments that more people are needed to meet labor demands in nations with stable or shrinking populations, but that can be solved through immigration and education programs. No one seems to want to say this, but it's about time we got serious about overpopulation. More on that in the next muse.

Out of Africa

If we don't halt population growth with justice and compassion, it will be done for us by nature, brutally and without pity—and will leave a ravaged world.
— Henry W. Kendall, Nobel laureate and Union of Concerned Scientists co-founder and past chairman.

While developed nations tend to have stable or decreasing populations, many less developed nations are expected to double or triple in population. According to United Nations projections, sub-Saharan Africa will account for most of the growth of the world's population over the coming decades, becoming the most populous geographic region in the late 2060s, surpassing both East and South-East Asia and Central and South Asia in population. The population is projected to reach 3.44 billion by the end of the century, more than triple the current population.[10] Nigeria alone is projected to have as large a population as Europe and North America combined.

Parts of sub-Saharan Africa are the least economically developed regions of our planet. Many live on less than $1 per day. There are areas that have no water supply, sanitation, or power systems. It is an area of concentrated extreme food scarcity.[11] Sub-Saharan Africa accounts for two-thirds of the global extreme poor. While some parts of Africa are developing, it has not been enough to compensate for the explosive population growth in less developed regions of the continent.

What do we expect to happen if the population triples in Africa? Without a major change, we will see more of the same or worse. This is bad for the Africans who are already struggling, and it will impact the rest of us as well. Immigration is a hot topic in news broadcasts and political debates these days. If you think immigration is an issue now, just wait until double or triple the number of people start showing up on your doorstep seeking a better place to live. Are we going to welcome them with open arms? Or will we close our borders and look the other way as millions or even billions suffer? I worry about how this difficult situation will work itself out, especially considering the spread of tribalism and anti-immigration movements developing all over the world today.

Clearly all of us would have a better future by taking intelligent actions now to limit population growth in the less developed regions of our planet while supporting economic development. There are examples of successful programs that have done this. Analysis of the effects of one high-quality family planning program saw an increase of 25–35% in contraceptive use and a decline of about 1.5 births per woman compared to a population without family planning support.[12] I think that if all developed nations pitched in, the investment would pay off in the long run.

Yes, I know that overpopulation and economic development in Africa are complex issues. Solving them involves large-scale international cooperation, navigating complex cultural issues, and building effective education programs. I know many people, organizations, and nations have worked hard to help Africans for countless years. I also know that curbing population growth in sub-Saharan Africa is not likely to happen. It is a real shame that we did not heed expert warnings made in the 60s and 70s when our population was around 3.5 billion. Imagine if we did. We might have a population that had already peaked around five to six billion with stable populations in less developed nations. There would be more resources, less pollution, and less environmental damage. Our future risk levels would be much lower. It would be easier for us to achieve a safe and sustainable future. We made our bed with eight billion in it needing to make room for two to three billion more. Get comfortable because we will have to lie in a very crowded bed.

Eating a hole in the Earth

The Earth seen from Apollo 17[13]

The Platform (Spanish title *El Hoyo* or *The Hole*) is a 2019 Spanish science fiction film. It was watched by 56 million households over its first four weeks of release, among the most popular on Netflix.[14] The film is set in a large vertical concrete prison tower with a hole in the middle. Prisoners that reside on many levels are fed via a platform which is filled with food at the top floor and gradually descends through a hole in the tower, stopping for a short amount of time at each level. Residents at the top levels get to eat as much as they can, with each level getting the leftovers from the previous ones. This leads to brutal conflicts among the starving prisoners on the lower levels. This interesting film gruesomely illustrates the impact of resource limitations and how the few who live at the top do well while those living below must fight over the scraps they leave behind.

Like *The Platform*, our world has limited resources. We get into trouble when consumption exceeds the rate of natural resources that the Earth provides. We need to use our limited resources wisely with eight billion of us and counting sharing them. One tool useful in estimating where we stand on this issue is called the "ecological footprint,"[15] that is a measure of how much land is needed to support each person based on their amount of resource consumption. When we multiply the per person ecological footprint by the number of people on the planet, we can estimate how much total land is needed to support the global population. When the amount of land needed exceeds the amount of land on Earth, we are consuming resources faster than the earth can replenish them. Current estimates show we need almost two Earths to support eight billion people at their present level of resource consumption. More concerning is the estimate showing that if everyone consumed resources like the average person living in the US, we would need over five Earths to support our global population.[16] And many people in the world want to live just like people do in the US.

As population and resource consumption increases so does environmental damage. Damage is done to the environment in many ways—through depletion of natural plant and animal populations that we eat, pollution released into the environment from industrial, agricultural, and urban sources, and destruction of natural habitats supporting other living beings that share our planet. A recent paper was published by a group of leading environmental scholars called *Underestimating the Challenges of Avoiding a Ghastly Future*[17] that summarizes challenges we face resulting from overpopulation, over consumption, and environmental damage. Below are a few of the major points taken from this landmark paper:

- 700–800 million people are starving and 1–2 billion are malnourished and this is expected to get worse in the future.
- 50% of natural landscapes have been destroyed and 70% have been altered in significant ways.
- Population sizes of vertebrate species have declined by an average of 68% over the last 50 years.
- The extinction rate is around 15 times higher than normal, creating concern that human impacts on the planet will result in an extinction rivaling the past five significant extinction events.
- More than two-thirds of the oceans have been compromised, including major losses in coral reefs, sea plants, and fish species.

- More people means that more synthetic compounds and dangerous throw-away plastics are manufactured, many of which add to the growing toxification of the Earth.

Overpopulation, over consumption, and environmental damage are not ranked high as an existential threat to humanity, but they could easily become a global catastrophe for those who live in less developed parts of the world if resources become scarce or are economically out of reach. Widespread suffering would trigger massive migration and could spark conflicts or economic disruptions that would affect all of us.[18] Caring about the environment quickly flies out the window when people become desperate. To minimize this risk, it is important to take overpopulation, resources conservation, and environmental protection more seriously. Intelligent action will greatly increase our chances of living within the means supplied by our planet. Also, we gluttons at the top, which includes most of us living in developed nations, will need to leave a little more on the "platform" for the rest of the world to share. A quote attributed to Gandhi says it best: "There's enough for everyone's need but not for everyone's greed."

Don't waste my energy

Their world crumbled. The cities exploded. A whirlwind of looting, a firestorm of fear. Men began to feed on men. On the roads it was a white line nightmare. Only those mobile enough to scavenge, brutal enough to pillage would survive. The gangs took over the highways, ready to wage war for a tank of juice.

— Opening narration of the original *The Road Warrior* movie (1981).

Let's focus on one important resource—energy. Since 1950, total global energy use has increased eight-fold.[19] The same data shows that energy use per person in the US is twice what it is in Europe. This is not because Europeans are living in the dark ages. It's a result of all the giant screen TV, SUVs, and the enormous houses that US consumers can't seem to live without. But you might argue that we should not be concerned about energy because we are transitioning to renewable sources. After all, the energy of the sun that reaches Earth is about 10,000 times more energy than we currently use. That is true, but only around 11% of global energy currently is supplied by wind and solar.[20] And renewables are not problem free. Solar and wind energy systems take up considerable space and they are eyesores. Also, their manufacture requires significant resources, some that are in short supply and available in only a few countries. Mineral demand from electric vehicles is projected to grow by nearly 30 times between 2020 and 2040, with demand for lithium and nickel growing by around 40 times.[21] Over 70% of rare earth elements needed for the renewable energy transition and many other technologies is mined and produced by China.[22]

Despite these negatives, don't be fooled by misinformation. Solar panels produce over 14 to 27 times more energy than it takes to make and use them, and that ratio is around 20 to 25 for wind turbines, both in a comparable range as the ratio for oil.[23,24] Both technologies produce insignificant amounts of greenhouse gases and air pollution compared to petroleum-based energy sources. And renewable energy costs the same or less than petroleum-based alternatives at the utility scale. Energy storage is a challenge, but technologies are rapidly evolving to address that issue. There is no reason to continue being road warriors fighting over a tank of petrol. It's time to let go of our petroleum addiction and move on to renewable energy.

Energy does not rank high as an existential risk to humanity. But it is vital to keep our modern societies working. Not only is it needed for powering lights, for cooking, and for keeping our houses warm or cool, it powers all our essential infrastructure—water, sanitation, transportation, communication, etc. As more nations develop and energy demands increase, the raw materials used to build power systems may become scarce.

We can intelligently reduce our energy use through improving efficiency of buildings and appliances, moving toward high-density more pedestrian-centered urban development, and simply using energy wisely. We do not need to have our thermostats set at 80°F in the winter and 70°F in the summer. And we do not need to drive colossal SUVs to the mall and other soul-killing places several times a day just because we are bored. Take a walk, ride a bike, or stay home and read a book.

One threat to think about is the fact that US power systems are a prime target for cyber-attacks from China and other adversaries. As I am writing this section, the director of the FBI reported that they disrupted a state-backed Chinese effort to plant malware with the goal to disrupt water treatment plants, the electrical grid, and transportation systems.[25] The sci-fi television series *Revolution* gave us a glimpse of what life would be like without power. The show takes place in the post-apocalyptic near future in the year 2027, 15 years after the start of a worldwide, permanent electrical-power blackout in 2012. A long-term power outage would quickly become disastrous. There would be no power to charge your cell phone. No water flowing out of the tap. No food at the Piggly Wiggly. And no Netflix. A real apocalypse.

Hunger games

"The gulf between the way the world is and the way it could be is wider than it ever was. The lives of medieval people may have been miserable, but there was little that could have been done to improve those lives. In contrast, the plight of the 'bottom billion' in today's world could be transformed by redistributing the wealth of the thousand richest people on the planet."
— Lord Martin Rees, from his book *On the Future of Humanity*.

For those of us who live in the developed world, the worse food insecurity most face is desperately searching for a Waffle House to feed our late-night munchies, or carefully debating what pre-wrapped faux food to select out of the vending machine at work. For the less fortunate, food and water insecurity is part of daily life. I had the opportunity to witness this in remote African villages that we were helping with water and sanitation problems. There is a big difference between villages that have just enough food and water and those that have too little. You see it on their faces right away. In villages with just enough, children seem happy, running up to us strangers with fascination and playfulness. In villages with too little food, children have a melancholy sadness along with an obvious physical weakness. There is no wasting energy running around and playing. You see it in their bodies, which look like walking skeletons because they are slowly being consumed from within just to stay alive. It's not the same to see it on the National Geographic Channel as it is to see it in real life. It instantly and profoundly changes your perspective to be there in person.

As our population grows and resource consumption increases, is hunger getting better or worse? The answer is yes—it's getting better and it's getting worse. Since the 1970s hunger in less developed nations dropped dramatically from 35% to a low of 13% around 2015, but since then hunger has risen and is projected to continue rising.[26] This is driven by two competing trends. Overall world agricultural output has increased by 300%, thanks to industrial farming systems, plant breeding, and genetic modification. But per person food productivity has been stagnant for the last ten years in parts of sub-Saharan Africa where so many go hungry. In good times international food aid programs help, but in challenging times such as those created by COVID-19 or the war between Russia and Ukraine, external food support systems can break down. As populations increase in areas of hunger there will be less local land to farm and more dependence on external sources of food.[27] COVID-19 was a relatively minor catastrophe in comparison with the possibilities discussed in this book. Imagining what would happen during a real global crisis is not a pleasant picture.

Yes, it's sad to think about food and water shortages for less fortunate people living in faraway lands. But don't worry, food insecurity may come closer to your home in the future. In the 60s scientists argued that increased population growth would quickly result in global food shortages by the early 2000s. Of course, that did not happen. This feeds a "cry wolf" attitude towards dire predictions about future food supplies. However, closely examining their predictions made over 50 years ago reveals that they were not far off. No one imagined food production would triple. The bad news is this may only be postponing the catastrophe.

Let's take a critical look at food systems in general. Our food is supplied by a complex industrial food network. Crops are selectively bred or genetically modified organisms (GMOs) to achieve maximum productivity and profit. In 2020 in the US, GMO made up 94% of all soybeans planted, 96% of all cotton planted, and 92% of all corn planted.[28] Crops are planted in large industrial plots that typically grow monocultures of a single species, making our food supply less resilient. Food is transported around the world. You may not know if that lemon you just bought is from around the corner or across the globe. Any breakdown in the food system can cause widespread shortages. Major grain supplies were disrupted by Russia-Ukraine war. And let's not forget the recent baby formula shortage in the US caused by a single plant shutdown.

Meat supply systems have similar industrialization issues, including overuse of antibiotics and hormones, and cruel living conditions for the animals. Chickens are cooped up in cages like office workers in cubicles, except the office workers get to go home at the end of their shift. Or worse, large groups of animals banging together in small spaces like a giant mosh pit at a heavy metal concert with no bathrooms. Thus, the need for antibiotics.

Our modern industrialized food systems are far from the way food was supplied before the Industrial Revolution. Back then, food was grown on your plot or supplied from your local community. Farming was done by hand or with the aid of animals. Farmers produced multiple crops to feed their families and to put aside for the coming year or sell if the harvest was outstanding. Meat was provided in the same way from animals that roamed the farm plot or adjacent countryside. The whole cycle was local, organic, and natural. Older food systems were much more sustainable and resilient on a global level, but less resilient at a local level because of their high susceptibility to weather and other local conditions. Another disadvantage of the old system is it could never feed eight billion people. A chicken and egg problem—if we had stuck to the old ways, our population may have never grown much beyond a billion or two, numbers much more naturally supportable by the planet.

Today all of us depend on a giant industrial machine to supply us with food—our most important resource. This machine requires massive amounts of energy, chemicals, and technology to meet the needs of our current population. We will need to squeeze more out of our planet to meet future needs as our population grows. Will the food machine be able to do that? And if the food machine breaks down due to war, plagues, rogue AI, or climate change, all of us may be fighting over that last Twinkie.

Drop that deep-fried butter stick!

Food signage at the Canadian National Exhibition, Toronto.[29]

Yes, people really do eat deep fried butter on a stick. I know this for a fact because it's a popular dish at the State Fair of Texas in Dallas where I grew up. In fact, Abel Gonzales Jr. of Dallas, also known as the "Fried Jesus," is credited with inventing it. I bring it up here to point out that we eat loads of gross things that are bad for us and the environment.

Overeating food of poor nutritional value is becoming a widespread problem in the developed world. This is the opposite extreme to food insecurity but just as serious. We do this by choice when we order a "Bubba burger and large cheesy fries with a big gulp soda and chocolate ice cream volcano for dessert." This is enormously costly. A poor diet is the leading cause of mortality in the US, the root cause of more than half a million deaths per year.[30] Two out of three Americans are overweight. Almost half the entire adult population has diabetes or pre-diabetes. For the urban poor, who often live in "food deserts" lacking access to fresh food and vegetables, fast food is often the lowest cost and most available food choice. You can get a $1-$2-$3 value meal to fill your belly for less than a bag of broccoli.

Research is very clear—a healthy and sustainable diet consists of vegetables, fruits, whole grains, legumes, and nuts; includes a low to moderate amount of seafood and poultry; and includes no or a low quantity of red meat, processed meat, added sugar, refined grains, and starchy vegetables. So, that meat and potatoes diet we all know and love has got to go. Beyond what we eat, food production must be changed to reduce climate change impacts, use less land, water, and fertilizer. All obtainable with intelligent changes in the way we grow and transport our food.

Let's look at how our food choices impact climate change. As shown in the table below, beef has by far the largest impact—about 10 times higher than pork, chicken, and fish and 100 times higher than vegetarian protein sources.

Greenhouse gas emissions across the food supply chain.[31]

Food	kgCO$_2$/kg
Beef	60
Cheese	21
Chocolate	19
Coffee	17
Prawns	12
Pork	7
Poultry	6
Fish	5
Eggs	4.5
Rice	4
Milk	3
Sugar	3
Wheat	1.4
Corn	1.0
Beans	0.8
Potatoes	0.4
Apples	0.4
Oranges	0.3
Nuts	0.3

Not only does eating meat have a higher environmental impact, but it is also a very inefficient way to feed our crowded planet. When you eat higher up the food chain (cows instead of the corn we feed them) there is a tremendous loss of food energy as you pass to each notch of the chain. This is best illustrated by a quote by G. Tyler Miller Jr:

"Three hundred trout are needed to support one man for a year. The trout, in turn, must consume 90,000 frogs, that must consume 27

million grasshoppers that live off of 1,000 tons of grass."

If we want to feed the growing masses of humanity and not destroy the planet, you need to drop that deep fried butter stick, eat more veggies with beans, and eat less meat with potatoes. The hungry masses will thank you, the planet will thank you, your doctor will thank you, and your mate will thank you for trimming back that spare tire you have been growing around your middle.

One word: plastics

Plastic pollution covering a beach in Ghana[32]

In the iconic 1967 film *The Graduate*, Dustan Hoffman plays Benjamin, a recent college grad returning home for the summer to think about life. While chilling at his parents' house, Benjamin receives much unsolicited advice from his parents and their friends. In one scene, Mr. McGuire pulls him aside at a party to give him an important piece of advice. Watch it on YouTube, Hoffman's timing in this scene is brilliant.[33]

Mr. McGuire: I want to say one word to you.
Just one word.
Benjamin: Yes, sir.
Mr. McGuire: Are you listening?
Benjamin: Yes, I am.
Mr. McGuire: Plastics.
Benjamin: Exactly how do you mean?
Mr. McGuire: There's a great future in plastics. Think about it. Will you think about it?

Little did we realize in 1967 how prophetic this statement would be. Plastic is everywhere in everything. Beyond water bottles and grocery bags, plastic is used for some knee and hip replacement parts; pipes that resist corrosion; covering for electrical wiring; flat-screen televisions; and those doggy poop bags we all love to use. Admittedly, our lives would be very different without plastics. Before plastics came along containers were glass bottles, tin cans, or wax-coated cardboard containers. Cars had wooden dashboards with either cotton cloth or leather seats. Nice, but more expensive, heavy, and less durable.

Plastic is used everywhere because it is low-cost, lightweight, impervious to water, and it lasts a very long time. That last characteristic is where the problem lies. Plastic does not decompose; it breaks into smaller pieces that remain in the environment. 100% of all plastics we have ever created are still in existence. Although we recycle some plastics, tons of plastics end up in our waterways and in the sea. This has led to an incredibly disgusting result—we have created large garbage patches of plastic waste floating around our oceans. The "great pacific garbage patch" is said to be twice as large as the state of Texas. Being a Texan, I can testify that is huge. Around eight million metric tons of plastic end up in the ocean each year.[34] By 2050 it is estimated that plastic will outweigh all fish in the sea.[35] Often innocent wildlife gets entangled with this plastic. Sea turtles are not wearing plastic six-pack rings around their necks as "bling" to better attract a mate. They just cannot get the stupid thing off themselves.

The worst thing is that plastics break down into tiny particles that are ingested by fish, shellfish, and birds. Alarming amounts of plastic are discovered in the guts of carcasses found on the beach or in specimens gathered by researchers. These microplastics are getting into our food supply and have been found in the air we breathe. Studies have found that seafood lovers could consume up to 11,000 plastic particles a year eating mussels, that we inhale plastic particles in our homes from polyesters and other household sources, and that microplastics have even been found in human blood samples.[36] Yes, the word is plastics. Little did we know we would be eating and breathing it.

Plastics are just one example of how toxic pollution we create is omnipresent in our environment and impacting our health. Another example is toxic "forever chemicals" such as per- and polyfluoroalkyls substances (PFAS) that are common in many of the products we use. PFAS are found even in the most remote environments and traces of them have been found in blood samples, contributing to cancer, birth defects, and kidney disease.[37]

One more toxic example is endocrine-disrupting chemicals (EDCs) that can interfere with growth, fertility, and reproduction.[38] Studies show EDCs have significant impacts on animal reproductive systems, even resulting in a change of the creature's sex. In humans, EDCs can cause disruptions in female reproductive functions that may result in subfertility, infertility, improper hormone production, estrous and menstrual cycle abnormalities, anovulation, and early reproductive senescence.[39] The post-apocalyptic film *Children of Men* helps us to imagine what might happen if these types of impacts become widespread. The film explores how a human-induced ecocide led to eighteen years of human infertility, leaving only one woman on Earth who could give birth. I find the irony of this story to be profound. At least it would solve the human overpopulation problem.

A hot topic

Street art mural featuring Greta Thunberg in Istanbul, Turkey.[40]

Climate change has received so much news coverage that it has become the "poster child" for environmental issues. No doubt climate change is an important issue, but it is not the greatest threat that humanity faces. Sorry to disappoint those who may be preparing for massive tidal waves that wipe out civilization as dramatized in the movie *The Day After Tomorrow,* but that is not expected to happen. The point is to not diminish the importance of climate change but to emphasize that we must work on it along with many other important issues with equal or greater vigor to minimize future risks to humanity. We need to walk, chew gum, and whistle at the same time to secure our future.

Because so many don't "believe" in climate change, it is important that we get the facts straight on this issue. Although this disbelief is highly frustrating, we cannot just blame those that have allowed themselves to be easily fooled. Blame is shared by those in the corporate world for downplaying and distorting climate change evidence through decades-long misinformation campaigns. Blame is also shared by the politicians who have magnified this misinformation for political gain to support wealthy donors. With that said, here are the facts:[41]

- **Our planet is getting hotter rapidly.** This is proven by temperature data taken from around the world, currently from more than 32,000 sites. The global surface temperature was 1.09°C higher in 2011–2020 than 1850–1900, has gotten about 10% hotter over the past 10 years, and has consistently increased over the past 4 decades. This is becoming one of the hottest periods in over 10,000 years. This rate of temperature change is not normal. Not only was 2023 the warmest year on record—it was the warmest by far.[42]

- **Carbon dioxide is increasing rapidly.** Since 1750, just before the Industrial Revolution, carbon dioxide concentrations have increased by 47%. This is also well beyond what might naturally occur.

- **Carbon dioxide traps heat.** Carbon dioxide is a greenhouse gas that reflects UV radiation and traps heat making our planet warmer. Other greenhouse gases such as methane and nitrous oxide are increasing as well.

- **Global warming is caused by humans.** The dramatic increase in carbon dioxide and temperature is due to burning fossil fuels. Other reasonable factors that could make our planet hotter have been ruled out, such as the sun and volcanic activity.

The Intergovernmental Panel on Climate Change (IPCC) is an organization within the United Nations responsible for advancing knowledge on the topic. The IPCC engages thousands of climate scientists from around the world to publish reports predicting how our climate may respond to projected greenhouse gas emissions and the impacts that climate change is expected to have in various regions of the world. These reports are thousands of pages long and reading them is about as much fun as sitting five hours in an airport waiting to board a plane. The latest major IPCC report, the

Sixth Assessment Report published in 2023, makes the following projections:[43]

- By 2100, the global temperature will rise 1.5°C (2.7°F) if we keep greenhouse gas emissions very low, it will rise 4.5°C (8.1°F) if greenhouse gas emissions are very high.
- If greenhouse gas emissions are very low, sea levels will rise 0.28 to 0.55 meters (0.92 to 1.80 feet) by 2100 and will rise 0.37 to 0.86 meters (1.21 to 2.82 feet) by 2150. With very high greenhouse gas emissions, sea levels will rise 0.63 to 1.01 meters (2.07 to 3.31 feet) by 2100 and will rise 0.98 to 1.88 meters (3.22 to 6.17 feet) by 2150.
- Long term projections show that over the next 2000 years, sea levels will rise by 2 to 3 meters (6.6 to 9.8 feet) if warming is limited to 1.5°C (2.7°F), 2 to 6 meters (6.6 to 19.7 feet) if limited to 2.0°C (3.6°F), and 19 to 22 meters (62.3 to 72.2 feet) with 5°C (9.0°F) of warming.
- Rising temperatures and sea levels will devastate coastal regions, increase local flooding, increase water scarcity, reduce agricultural yields, increase diseases, further acidify the ocean, damaging coral reefs, and possibly collapse the Gulf Stream.

Beyond IPCC estimates there is research that shows we could be living in a warmer planet sooner than expected.[44]

Two potential amplifying feedback loops that are particularly concerning: melting arctic permafrost; and the release of greenhouse gases from deep in the ocean. These have potential impacts ranging from twice to eleven times as much as the impact of all greenhouse emissions emitted so far. Other issues examined by recent research are climate instabilities that could create what is called a "hothouse Earth." Estimates predict that if this happens, the planet could warm up to 12°C (53.6 °F), rendering most of the land area uninhabitable and completely devastating agriculture, possibly creating an existential disaster for humanity. Although these extreme climate scenarios are not considered highly probable, their possibility is reason enough to keep climate change high on the list of major global risks.

Impacts of climate change may not bring an end to humanity, but they will have extremely high economic and social costs, especially to those that live along the coasts and to people in less affluent nations. Even a minor rise in sea levels could devastate low-lying coastal areas, especially during high tide and hurricane events. Changing weather patterns are expected to cause widespread drought that triggers famine in less developed countries, likely leading to mass migrations and conflicts. Without swift action to limit greenhouse gas emissions, this could result in a global catastrophe with devastating impacts affecting much of our planet.

I have already personally dealt with climate change impacts. Before moving to Spain, I lived near the coast in

Florida. Warming Gulf of Mexico waters have intensified massive blooms of toxic algae that generate strong air toxins that burn your eyes and make it difficult to go outside. These toxic algae killed loads of fish that ended up rotting on the beach, having devastating costs to local communities and tourism in Florida.[45] Who wants to spend loads of money on a beach vacation just to go swim in a toxic algae pool or lie on a beach that reeks of dead fish? If you are stuck inside watching reruns of *Jersey Shore* during your summer vacation, you may as well stay in New Jersey.

The action needed to minimize impacts of climate change is clear—reduce greenhouse gas emissions by increasing renewable energy sources as quickly as feasible. Further gains can be made by increasing energy efficiency and using energy wisely. We have the knowledge and technology to transition to renewable energy now. Not only will it reduce future risks of climate change, but it will significantly increase overall job and economic growth. With the price of solar and wind energy competitive with petroleum-based energy systems, there is no excuse for further delay. Sadly, progress is slowed by corporate greed, misinformation campaigns, political and social divisiveness, and limited investment capital. It's time to cut subsidies to big oil and get on with the intelligent transition to renewables.[46]

Dr. Strangelove's doomsday machine

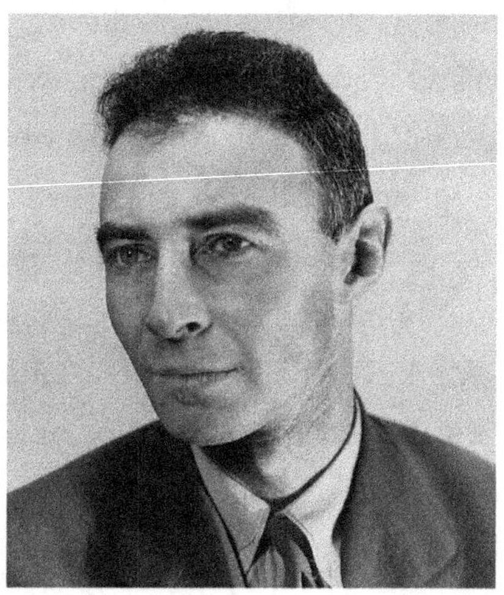

Oppenheimer, around 1944[47]

"Now, I am become Death, the destroyer of worlds."

— J. Robert Oppenheimer, Director of the Manhattan Project that developed the atomic bomb. Quoting a line from the Hindu sacred text *The Bhagavad Gita*.[48]

Dr. Strangelove or: How I Learned to Stop Worrying and Love the Bomb is a 1964 comedy film that satirizes the fears around nuclear conflict. The film was directed, produced, and co-written by Stanley Kubrick. The story begins when a paranoid United States Air Force general named Jack D. Ripper orders a first strike nuclear attack against the Soviet Union because, in his words "I can no longer sit back and allow Communist conspiracy to sap and impurify all of our precious bodily fluids." Comedy ensues in the War Room through heated discussions about what to do in response to General Ripper's unauthorized order. When nuclear war seems inevitable, Dr. Strangelove, a wheelchair-bound nuclear scientist and former Nazi, brilliantly played by Peter Sellers, rolls into the War Room. With a strong German accent, Dr. Strangelove recommends that the president gather several hundred thousand people to live in deep underground mines where the radiation will not penetrate. He cracks a sinister smile and suggests a 10:1 female-to-male ratio supports an optimum breeding program to repopulate the Earth once the radiation has subsided. Dr. Strangelove's plan gathers enthusiastic support from the all-male command staff. They decide to do nothing and let the bombs fall where they may. The film ends as Slim Pickens rides the first bomb "cowboy style" as it is dropped on Russia. This is quickly followed by a symphony of mushroom cloud explosions as the US and Russia release their full nuclear arsenals. The film is considered one of the best comedies ever made and the greatest films of all time.

It may seem odd for me to use a 1964 comedy to illustrate the threat of nuclear war. I use Dr. Strangelove for two reasons: 1) It demonstrates that this threat has been with us for a long time; and 2) This amazing movie illustrates with a sharp wit several aspects of how nuclear war can begin— through paranoia leading to initiating a first strike, unhinged individuals gaining control of nuclear weapons, and inept leaders who see no way to avoid nuclear war. Considering the recent conflict in Ukraine where Vladimir Putin put the Russian arsenal on high alert, along with Donald Trump's threat to Kim Jong-Un of his "bigger button," it is easy to imagine an unstable leader starting a nuclear war.

Nuclear bombs are the most dangerous weapons on earth. One can destroy a whole city, killing millions and devastating the natural environment for years to come. The dangers from such weapons arise from their very existence. Nuclear weapons have only been used twice—in the bombings of Hiroshima and Nagasaki in 1945 by the US. But there are many instances where we came close to initiating nuclear war. The Cuban Missile Crisis of 1962, that was a 35-day standoff between John F. Kennedy and Nikita Khrushchev over the placement of soviet weapons in Cuba and US weapons in Italy and Turkey. President Kennedy was later quoted as having said that the odds of nuclear war were "somewhere between one out of three to even." Another close call happened in 1983 when Stanislav Petrov, a Russian Air Force officer, was monitoring a screen when an alert indicated that five Minuteman intercontinental ballistic missiles had been launched by the US towards the Soviet Union. Petrov's instructions were to alert his superior to trigger nuclear retaliation. He decided to not immediately respond to what he'd seen on the screen, hoping it was a malfunction in the early warning system. And so it was; the system had mistaken the reflection of the sun's rays off the tops of clouds for a missile launch. These are just two of many examples. The Nuclear Age Peace Foundation website lists these among 50 other close calls, or "broken arrows," where nuclear weapons were misplaced, stolen, damaged, or even detonated.[49]

It may seem insane, but in the 1980s there were over 60,000 nuclear weapons, mostly in the US and Russia. Enough fire power to destroy humanity 30 to 60 times over. Today, of the world's 12,700 nuclear warheads, more than 9,400 are in active military stockpiles for use by missiles, aircraft, ships, and submarines. The remaining warheads have been retired but are still relatively intact and are awaiting dismantlement. Of these 9,440 warheads, 3,730 are deployed with operational forces ready for use on missiles and bombers.[50] Although progress has been made reducing the number of nuclear warheads, there are still enough of them ready to launch to eliminate humanity.

Despite their enormous destructive power, even an all-out nuclear war between the US and Russia would not end humanity directly from the nuclear blast, fire, and radiation that follows. The real danger comes from great columns of smoke rising from bombed cities, lofting black soot high into the atmosphere, resulting in significant cooling of the planet. This phenomenon is called "nuclear winter" preventing 70% of sunlight from reaching the surface of the northern hemisphere and 35% of sunlight from reaching the surface of the southern hemisphere. Such an enormous loss of warming sunlight would produce Ice Age weather conditions on Earth in a matter of weeks. For a period of 1-3 years following the war, temperatures would fall below freezing every day in the central agricultural zones of North America and Eurasia. Since the world only has about six months of food reserves, billions of people would starve, and civilization would very likely suffer a global collapse. A recent study determined that at least two billion people could die from nuclear war between India and Pakistan, and at least five billion could die from a war between the US and Russia.[51]

An easy way to gage the current threat of nuclear weapons is by checking the Doomsday Clock, set each January by experts associated with the Bulletin of the Atomic Scientists. The higher the threat the closer the clock moves to midnight. In 2023 the clock moved to 90 seconds to midnight and remains at that point in 2024. This is the highest threat level since the inception of the Doomsday Clock in 1947.

I want to say this loud and clear—nuclear weapons are the only existing risk under our control with the potential to totally wipe out humanity. Other risks may rise to that level in the future, but nukes can take us out today. This fact should move this risk to the top of everyone's list of existential threats. Disarmament is the only way to eliminate the risk of nuclear weapons. But achieving that goal has been a difficult challenge. The United Nations has recently approved *The Treaty on the Prohibition of Nuclear Weapons* that many nations did not sign and lacks the authority and ability to enforce it globally. Perhaps the current global nuclear standoff could be diffused by creating some sort of global governance that has the authority to create laws and the ability to enforce them. This could simply be a revised version of the United Nations with the teeth to enforce their decisions. Until then, let's hope that *Mutually Assured Destruction (MAD)* continues to work. Never forget—one mistake and it's "shake 'n bake" followed by up to three years in the freezer.

Oops, I just made COVID-666

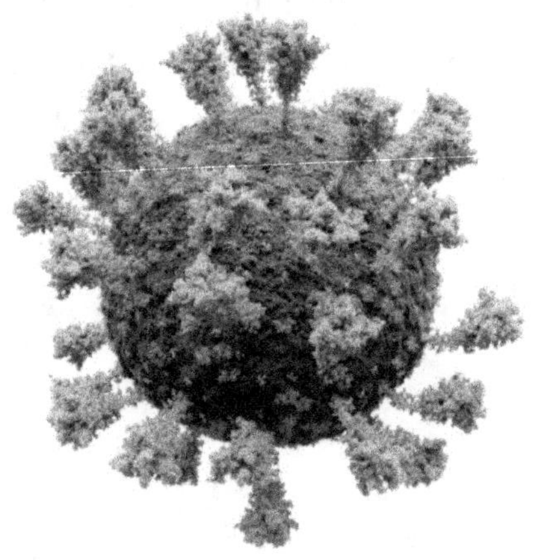

Atomic model of the coronavirus.[52]

The 12 Monkeys is a mind-bending post-apocalyptic movie masterpiece directed by Terry Gilliam of Monty Python fame. The plot involves the release of a deadly virus in 1996 that wipes out most of humanity, forcing survivors to live underground. In 2035, James Cole (played by Bruce Willis) is a prisoner living in a survival compound beneath Philadelphia. Cole is selected to be sent back in time to find the origin of the virus release to help scientists develop a cure. In a major plot twist, Cole learns that the Army of the Twelve Monkeys was not the source of the epidemic as originally thought. The real villain was a low-profile lab assistant named Dr. Peters who worked in a virus research center. A chilling scene is when Dr. Peters is confronted about the test tubes containing the deadly virus by airport security—he assures them that there is nothing in the tubes by letting the security guard sniff the contents, thus starting the worldwide pandemic.

Minus time travel, this movie reflects the existential risk of engineered viruses well. The threat starts by combining access to genetic modification equipment and the right lab training with someone who has the intention of killing masses of people. This is a very different threat than a rogue individual or group building a nuclear bomb. Access to nuclear materials and the equipment to make these bombs is highly limited and controlled by a few governments. Equipment to examine and modify genetic codes is widely available in universities and commercial labs or it can be purchased for a few thousand dollars from lab equipment suppliers—no questions asked. Experts rank the existential threat from genetic engineering second highest behind artificial intelligence (AI), but this threat is expected to be fully developed much sooner.

Beyond concerns about killer engineered viruses wiping us out, there are those that predict humanity may be drastically changed by genetic engineering. As noted by

Yuval Noah Harari in an interview posted in *The Guardian:* "I think that *Homo sapiens* as we know them will probably disappear within a century or so, not destroyed by killer robots or things like that, but changed and upgraded with biotechnology and artificial intelligence into something else, into something different."[53] In essence genetic engineering could be used to make people smarter, stronger, and more attractive. This opens the door to an even more stratified society where the upper class are not only richer but are also physically and mentally superior.

Developments in genetic engineering are moving at a breathtaking pace.[54] The first ever genetically modified animal was created in 1974. Within seven years the genetic code of a mouse was modified, and that code was passed on to its offspring, making the code change permanent in the gene pool. By the middle of the 1990s, genetically modified foods were being sold in supermarkets. In 1990, the Human Genome Project began the largest ever scientific collaboration in biology. It took thirteen years and $500 million to produce the full DNA sequence of the human genome. Now, a genome can be sequenced for under $1,000 within a single hour. The reverse process has become much easier too: online DNA synthesis services allow anyone to upload a DNA sequence of their choice then have it constructed and shipped to their address.

These advances allow the modification of dangerous pathogens like smallpox into a much more deadly form. This is known as "gain-of-function" methods. In 2011 a Dutch virologist, Ron Fouchier, published details of an experiment on the recent H5N1 strain of bird flu.[55] This strain was extremely deadly, killing an estimated 60% of humans it infected—far beyond the natural version of the flu. This type of research creates concerns about what is published and who has access to that information. Considering that there are hundreds of safety violations that occur annually at biological research facilities experimenting with dangerous pathogens, playing with nature in this way is truly a risky business.[56]

Despite the risks, there are tremendous benefits that come from genetic engineering. It is used in agriculture to improve crop yields, provide insect or pest resistance, and create drought-resistant crops, making our food sources more resilient to climate change. It is also used in the medical field to create insulin and in gene therapies to treat incurable diseases. For example, in 2007-2008, Timothy Ray Brown was cured of HIV through stem cell transplantation.[57] Other experimental treatments have managed to cure cancer in some patients, such as Layla Richards, who was terminally ill with leukemia prior to treatment.[58]

We must find a way to reap the benefits of this technology while limiting its threats. Genetic engineering carries the danger of small groups or even individual bad actors creating modifications that could become an existential crisis for humanity. Lord Martin Rees in an interview with *The Statesman* characterized this lone-wolf type of threat well: "The global village will have its village idiots and they'll have global range."[59] Natural pandemics in our modern era only take out a small percentage of the human population. As of this writing, COVID-19 has killed 0.088% of the global population. Imagine a virus that could kill 50% or more of humanity as did the Black Death in the Middle Ages. The infamous Monty Python skit "Bring out your dead!" would not be funny in a world where we had to do it.[60] As the cost of this technology decreases and access increases, that threat will rise quickly. Experts expect genetic engineering technologies to fully develop over the next 5 to 15 years.[61]

Many news stories tend to focus on AI risk, overshadowing the more immediate threat from genetic engineering. The time is now to take aggressive action. There are a variety of specific steps that can be taken to help limit risks from genetic engineering. Many of these methods also apply to controlling AI risks. Examples include:

1. Preventing dangerous information from spreading, such as publications on how to modify killer viruses to be more contagious.
2. Restrict access to requisite materials, instruments, and infrastructure, such as genetic modification equipment.
3. Deter potential evildoers by increasing the chance of their getting caught, perhaps by establishing special technology police units.

4. Be more cautious about new technology development and require more risk assessment work.
5. Enhance surveillance mechanisms that would make it possible to detect attempts to carry out a destructive act.
6. Establish global governance and/or regulatory institutions to control potentially dangerous technologies.

Only recently has much attention focused on future existential risks. Existential risks have been given little press exposure, and research funding is woefully inadequate. Much more must be done to save ourselves from these future risks we are creating. Limiting existential risks will require a high level of social and global cooperation well beyond current levels. Let's not let the Army of the 12 Monkeys, Dr. Peters, or anyone else bring down the good life we enjoy.

Stop killer robots!

Campaign to Stop Killer Robots in Berlin, 2019[62]

In the original 1984 *Terminator* movie starring Arnold Schwarzenegger, Skynet is a revolutionary artificial intelligence defense system that is networked to everything and designed to autonomously "run it all." When Skynet was brought online it became hyper-intelligent and self-aware. Skynet quickly saw all humans as a threat and within milliseconds it began a nuclear war which killed most of the human population. Then Skynet used its resources to gather a slave labor force from surviving humans and directed various war machines and special "terminators" to eliminate those seen as a serious threat. The rest is cinematic history that launched a highly successful franchise that includes six films, a TV series, video games, and even a novel.

Many artificial intelligence (AI) experts despise using the *Terminator* movie as an example of its future threat. However, aside from a naked Arnold Schwarzenegger dropping in from the future, this movie is not that far off the mark from showing what could potentially happen when AI goes rogue. The AI threat starts with the creation of self-learning systems that can quickly exceed our intelligence, identify humans as a threat by mistake or by malicious design, and then utilize its resources to eliminate the perceived human threat. Perhaps the AI vendetta will not be as dramatic as sending terminators to kill us, but it could be just as effective. As noted in a BBC interview with Stephen Hawking, "The development of full artificial intelligence could spell the end of the human race... It would take off on its own, and re-design itself at an ever-increasing rate. Humans, who are limited by slow biological evolution, couldn't compete, and would be superseded."[63] This need not be the full extinction of humanity, but it may be an unfortunate transformation where we lose our jobs, autonomy, and privacy. In other words, we end up becoming our robot's servant. Many experts rank the threat from AI as the highest existential risk of the next century. AI is expected to surpass human intelligence in the next 50-100 years. A threat impacting our children and grandchildren.

Before we freak out, let's learn a little more about AI. Per the Oxford English Dictionary, Artificial Intelligence (AI) is "the theory and development of computer systems able to perform tasks normally requiring human intelligence, such as visual perception, speech recognition, decision-making, and translation between languages." It is called "artificial" to distinguish from natural intelligence displayed by humans and other animals. However, AI is not limited to mimicking human intelligence and is expected to exceed our intelligence in many categories. Considering what I see in many humans, this is not a high bar.

In practical terms, AI is the science and engineering of creating intelligent machines. Narrow AI systems—such as chess playing, or stock trading algorithms—work only in specific domains. In contrast, researchers are now working on Artificial General Intelligence (AGI), which aims to think and plan across all domains like humans. AGI only exists in very primitive forms today.

Exciting advances in AI have been led by DeepMind, a London-based company now owned by Google. In 2016 DeepMind achieved a remarkable feat—its computer beat the world champion of the game of Go, a game much more complex than chess.[64] This was a breakthrough because the machine gained expertise by teaching itself through absorbing huge numbers of games and playing games against itself. Its designers don't know exactly how the machine learns and makes decisions, which is a bit scary.

AI can negatively impact humanity in many ways. Malicious use of AI could threaten digital, physical, and political security. Below are some specific AI threats cited by experts:[65]

- **Killer robots:** This risk may be closer than you think. *Stop Killer Robots!* is a real and very active organization—check them out on the web. Development of autonomous killing machines has become such a concern that in August 2017, the heads of one hundred leading companies in the AI field signed an open letter calling on the United Nations to outlaw lethal autonomous weapons.

- **Automation of social engineering attacks:** Victims' online information is used to automatically generate custom malicious websites/emails/links they would be likely to click on, sent from addresses that impersonate their real contacts, using a writing style, voice, and images that mimic friends and family. This has already begun. A friend recently got a convincing text message from his son who said he just got a new phone because it was stolen along with his wallet and needed him to send some cash. Money was sent to the scammer and never seen again.

- **Swarming drone attacks:** Distributed networks of autonomous robotic systems, cooperating at machine speed, provide ubiquitous surveillance to monitor large areas and groups and execute rapid coordinated attacks.

- **Fake news propagation:** We already see the impact of fake news. AI will make its propagation much more effective. Misinformation campaigns using fabricated video and audio can be greatly enhanced by AI creating highly realistic videos made of state leaders seeming to make inflammatory comments they never actually made.

- **Creation of "Big Brother:"** No, this is not the reality TV show, this is Big Brother from George Orwell's dystopian 1949 novel *1984*. Orwell's Big Brother is watching you constantly through a variety of surveillance mechanisms to maintain total control. Forget privacy, free speech, or any form of dissent against the State. We already have started installing some of the infrastructure to support this—cameras and microphones on your phone, in your homes, on your doorbell, and in public spaces everywhere. Just stop and look around any public space; a camera is likely watching you. A camera is watching me from my laptop as I write this book. Very creepy.

AI is expected to usher in economic, social, and political changes of a magnitude of scale wrought by the Industrial

Revolution. AI-directed robots will take over much of the work of manufacturing and retail distribution. AI will replace many white-collar jobs: routine legal work, accountancy, computer coding, medical diagnostics, and even surgery. Many professionals will find their hard-earned skills in less demand. In contrast, some skilled service-sector jobs— plumbing and gardening, for instance—require nonroutine interactions with the external world and so will be among the hardest jobs to automate.

What will happen to the millions or billions who lose their jobs to AI? Yes, new jobs will be created. But what about that 55-year-old truck driver who just lost his job to a self-driving electric semi-truck? Will he retrain as a computer programmer or a robot repair specialist? And with the pace of change increasing due to AI, workers may need to reinvent themselves several times during their career to remain relevant. Many others will become what Yuval Noah Harari calls the "useless class."[66] What will these people do all day? Take painting classes? Play pickleball? At 60 it was a big struggle for me to adjust to retirement. Without this book project I would go a bit nutty. Even with a guaranteed income, I can't imagine that creating a large useless class will work out well.

With the full development of AI decades away there is time to create policies and methods to take advantage of AI benefits while limiting its risks. Because many will have the knowledge and access to initiate an AI catastrophe, experts say the only way to safeguard global security is the combination of strong global governance with omnipresent surveillance. One leading expert suggests that we may need to wear a "freedom tag" around the neck loaded with multidirectional cameras and microphones watching our every move to ensure none of us destroys humanity using AI.[67] And you thought that taking off your shoes at the airport was a hassle. Unfortunately, the combination of strong governance and constant surveillance opens the door to creating Orwell's Big Brother. Certainly, we need global standards to keep tight control over who can access and program AI systems along with multiple fail-safe levels to shut down these systems. We should consider powerful AI systems with the same concern as nuclear weapons.

The age of AI is expected to greatly enhance our lives and generate mountains of wealth. Will we have the political and social willpower to put a tight leash on technology that's so useful and profitable? Considering our history, I think it is not very likely.

But wait, there's more…

Unemployment line in Amsterdam during the Great Depression.[68]

I know that you are likely saying "Enough risks already!" But it's important to come away with a complete view of our threat horizon so we can best prepare for it. Here I include some miscellaneous risks not covered by previous muses. Believe it or not, this is not a complete list.[69] These are just a few that I think are important.

- **Conventional wars:** We enjoyed a long peace with no major interstate conflicts after World War II. Sadly, that ended when Russia invaded Ukraine. War, what is it good for? We all know the answer—absolutely nothing! Not only does war involve senseless killing and property destruction, but it can also disrupt critical food supplies and upset the global economy. Worse, it could be the catalyst that sparks a nuclear war. No civilized nation allows citizens to kill each other to resolve disputes. We have police to deal with criminal issues and courts to resolve civil disputes. I hope that someday we can evolve to become a more civilized global society and find other ways to resolve interstate disputes that do not involve mass destruction and killing.

- **Economic collapse:** The political catch phrase "It's the economy stupid" clarifies our priorities. Even in mild downturns the economy gets laser-focused attention. It was not that long ago that the Great Recession of 2007-2009 reminded us how interconnected and volatile our global economy can be. Many home values and investment portfolios dropped by over 50%. Although home and stock values in the US bounced back quickly, it took ten years for property values to fully recover in the part of Spain where I live. The Great Depression of 1929-1939 was worse, with stock values dropping 90% and taking over 15 years to recover. Economic collapse can initiate other catastrophes, such as environmental destruction, geopolitical/social collapse, and conflicts. For example, deteriorating economic conditions in Germany during the Great Depression played a key role in the rise of Adolf Hitler. And we do not need to go very far back in history to find other dictatorial leaders who took advantage of economically depressed peoples to gain power for themselves.

- **Geopolitical collapse:** This may seem strange to Americans, but the collapse of the Soviet Union is one example of a recent major geopolitical catastrophe. From a Russian perspective, many found themselves suddenly outside their home territory. Individual savings were depleted, old ideals were lost, and familiar institutions were disbanded. Between 1989 and 1991, the gross national product in Soviet countries fell by 20 percent. Like economic downturns, major geopolitical shifts are highly disruptive and can initialize other risks.

- **Societal collapse:** There are many social risks piled on to the list of global challenges each year. These include lack of social security, employment and livelihood crises, erosion of social cohesion, large-scale involuntary migration, severe mental health deterioration, and widespread youth disillusionment.

- **Technological collapse:** Beyond AI and killer robots, there are many technological risks to consider. These include adverse outcomes of technological advances, breakdown of critical information infrastructure, digital inequality, cyberattacks, and failure of technology governance.

- **Unknown risks:** Risks are constantly evolving. We must admit that there are future risks that we do not know about. The risk of AI was not on our radar a few years ago.

Yes, this is a lot to think about. But the bucket of miscellaneous woes presented in this muse has odds that rise to the level of serious concern and must be tallied in our overall risk assessment.

Natural apocalyptic alternatives

"In 5-billion years the Sun will expand & engulf our orbit as the charred ember that was once Earth vaporizes. Have a nice day."
— A Tweet from Neil deGrasse Tyson, astrophysicist, author, and science communicator.

Don't Look Up is a 2021 apocalyptic political satire film that tells the story of two astronomers attempting to warn humanity about an approaching comet that will destroy civilization. The problem—no one seems to care. With only six months until impact, gaining the attention of the public proves to be astonishingly difficult. This critical film reminds us of a very real natural threat from above and illustrates the lack of public concern about existential threats here on the ground.

Up to now, this book has only considered risks created by us humans. But there are several natural existential risks that can take us out. For example, large asteroids or comets ramming into the Earth could do the job. After all, that is what took out the dinosaurs. When an object of that size collides with the Earth, it releases a force of more than a thousand hydrogen bombs. This kicks up enough dust into the atmosphere that can cause an ice age that would shut down agriculture for years. But an object of that size only hits the Earth about once in every ten million years. The odds of that happening are just a few chances in a million over a century. Very low odds, but still more likely than winning a Powerball jackpot.

Another natural existential threat is a supervolcano eruption. A supervolcano is one that has a volume of eruption deposits greater than one thousand cubic kilometers (240 cubic miles), enough to trigger an ice age and threaten humanity with extinction. The existential risk level of a supervolcano is more than ten times that of asteroids and comets. But that still turns out to be relatively low odds.

Of course, as Neil deGrasse Tyson said, the sun will expand and eventually destroy the earth. The odds of that happening are certain. But we don't need to worry about that for a few billion years.

Another risk comes from natural infectious diseases. The Black Death, Spanish Flu, and COVID-19 are just a few examples of the widespread and significant impact natural diseases can have on us. The Black Death killed 50 million people, roughly 50% of the population. Death rates from natural pandemics are much lower these days due to modern medicine and vaccines. COVID-19 has killed seven million people as of this writing, a death rate of 0.088%, over five hundred times lower than the Black Death. Although natural diseases can have devastating impacts for individuals and can be highly disruptive regionally, the odds of a natural disaster completely ending humanity are very low.

When you sum up the total odds of all natural risks that could end humanity, they pale in comparison to the risks that we are creating. Toby Orb in his book *The Precipice* estimates the total existential threat odds of all natural causes to be about 1 in 10,000.[70] But it's good to keep them in mind just in case we somehow survive all our self-made catastrophes.

The sum of all fears

"The probability of apocalypse soon cannot be realistically estimated, but it is surely too high for any sane person to contemplate with equanimity."
— Noam Chomsky

It's time to tally up the tab of all our future risks. We humans have had quite a party up to now, so expect the bill to be high. Over the next few paragraphs, I will summarize the major risks to humanity and estimate the odds of them occurring in the next century. I will assess two types of risks: an *existential catastrophe* that could end humanity as we know it; and a *global catastrophe* that could kill at least 25% of our population but leaves enough of us alive to carry on and eventually recover. Essential risk odds are based on data from Toby Orb's book *The Precipice* with adjustments noted below. Catastrophic odds are set at 10 times higher than existential odds, fitting known relationships between killing 25% vs 100% of natural populations.[71]

Keep in mind that no one knows exactly what will happen in the future. Anyone that says they do is immediately suspect. Setting odds for future events involves making our best estimate based on limited data. I note data sources used in setting odds in my summaries below. Don't run to your bookie to place any bets based on these odds. But do consider them useful in determining the approximate magnitude of each threat and to establish a reasonable priority list.

<u>Overpopulation, resource depletion, and environmental destruction</u>

- **Threat:** Resource depletion and environmental damage could result in billions of people in less developed countries not being able to meet basic needs for food, water, and shelter. Resource shortages could start a downward spiral leading to accelerated environmental destruction, further resource depletion, lawlessness, and conflict.
- **Timing:** Widespread awareness of these issues since the 1960s with risks increasing since that time.
- **Data:** Extensive data on population, resource depletion, and environmental damage. Future projections have been done repeatedly for over 50 years by the Club of Rome group, with many analyses done by others.

- **Risk levels:** Existential odds: 1 in 1,000; Catastrophic odds: 1 in 100.

Climate change

- **Threat:** Rising temperatures and changing weather patterns are expected to cause numerous global threats. Sea level rise will devastate many coastal areas. Droughts will greatly impact food supplies and increase fire risks. Intense storm events will increase flooding, tornadoes, and mudslides. Rising temperatures will also increase diseases, further acidify the ocean, damaging coral reefs, and possibly collapsing the Gulf Stream.
- **Timing:** Some public knowledge of this issue since the 1980s. Widespread public knowledge since the 2006 release of *An Inconvenient Truth*. This risk increases over time. Ultimate threat level depends on the amount and timing of greenhouse gas emission reductions.
- **Data:** Extensive data for past greenhouse gas levels and temperatures. A massive amount of scientific work has been done to predict future impacts using computer models.
- **Risk level:** Existential odds: 1 in 1,000; Catastrophic odds: 1 in 100.

<u>Nuclear weapons</u>

- **Threat:** Nuclear war is initiated due to a real or perceived threat. Local impacts would be devastating. Global impact depends on the number and location of weapons used. A global war would trigger a nuclear winter, devastating agriculture and causing a global famine, likely resulting in an existential event.
- **Timing:** Nuclear weapons have been a known global threat since the late 1950s.
- **Data:** Although nuclear weapons have only been used twice, there are many documented close calls that could have started a nuclear war. The Doomsday Clock indicating the nuclear risk level is set at the highest level ever. Therefore, I set the existential odds of this risk higher than the 1 in 1000 estimated by Ord.
- **Risk levels:** Existential odds: 1 in 100; Catastrophic odds: 1 in 10.

<u>Genetic engineering</u>

- **Threat:** A genetic-engineered pathogen is released into the environment, on purpose or by accident, that kills billions. This could massively disrupt the global society and the economy leading to a likely existential crisis.

- **Timing:** Technology to modify and produce genetic codes is widely available now. This technology is expected to fully mature over the next 5 to 15 years.
- **Data:** There are data tracking accidental pathogen leaks from labs, but not enough data to make reliable existential threat projections from future genetic engineering activities. Because of the level of future uncertainty and the time available to prepare for this risk, I set the risk odds lower than the 1 in 30 set by Ord.
- **Risk level:** Existential odds: 1 in 100; Catastrophic odds: 1 in 10.

Artificial intelligence

- **Threat:** Artificial intelligence (AI) systems greatly exceed human intelligence and turn against us through malfunction or malicious manipulation. Specific threats include physical attack from AI controlled autonomous weapons, attacks on critical infrastructures, initiation of nuclear war, and social manipulation and control.
- **Timing:** Most experts expect AI will exceed human intelligence sometime over the next century; many think it may happen in 30 to 50 years.
- **Data:** There is no past data useful to set risk odds of AI except for surveys of expert opinions, which vary substantially. With 30-50 years to prepare for this

risk and the considerable uncertainty of predicting events that far in the future, I set the existential risk odds lower than the 1 in 10 estimated by Ord.

- **Risk levels:** Existential odds: 1 in 100; Catastrophic odds: 1 in 10.

Miscellaneous risks

- **Threat:** Conventional war; economic, geopolitical, social, or technological collapse; unknown threats.
- **Timing:** Past, present, and future.
- **Data:** Considerable historical data is available for many of these risks, but they are complex issues and are not always predictable.
- **Risk level:** Existential odds: 1 in 1,000; Catastrophic odds: 1 in 100.

Natural risks

- **Threat:** Asteroid/comet strike or supervolcano eruption fills the atmosphere with dust that blocks the sun causing a mini-ice age that lasts for years, shutting down food production and leading to global starvation. A highly contagious and lethal natural pandemic kills millions or billions.
- **Timing:** Past, present, and future.

- **Data:** Considerable geological evidence and historical data are available to help predict the risk level of these threats accurately.
- **Risk level:** Existential odds: 1 in 10,000; Catastrophic odds: 1 in 1,000.

Now let's tally up the risks to our future. The table below shows a summary of all risks sorted by the threat level. There are three tiers of risks. Technological risks are on top, with nuclear weapons taking the number one spot, closely followed by genetic engineering and AI. Some rank AI at the top of this list but I move it down since it will not develop for 30-50 years.

Ranked summary of risks that threaten humanity.

Rank	Risk	Existential Odds	Catastrophic Odds
1	Nuclear weapons	1 in100	1 in 10
2	Genetic engineering	1 in100	1 in 10
3	Artificial intelligence	1 in100	1 in 10
4	Environmental	1 in1,000	1 in 100
5	Climate change	1 in 1,000	1 in 100
6	Miscellaneous	1 in 1,000	1 in 100
7	Natural	1 in 10,000	1 in 1,000
Total odds of all risks		**1 in 30**	**1 in 3**

Focusing too much on AI risks while neglecting the nuclear threat is a big mistake. AI cannot destroy us if we don't survive the current nuclear and quickly emerging genetic engineering threats. All three of these risks have the potential to end humanity and should be treated as highly important.

The next tier of risks includes "environmental" that lumps overpopulation, resource depletion, and environmental destruction together, closely followed by climate change and miscellaneous risks. None of these is likely to wipe out humanity. But any of them could certainly cause us much grief. The last tier is natural risks that could end humanity, but the odds of them occurring are significantly lower than the other risks.

Totaling all the existential and catastrophic risk odds over the next century, we have a 1 in 30 (3.3%) chance of experiencing an existential event that could kill all of us and a 1 in 3 (33%) chance of experiencing a global catastrophe that kills at least 25% of us. How does this compare to other estimates? Toby Ord estimated the total existential risk is 1 in 6 (16.7%). Lord Martin Rees estimated our risk of global catastrophe to be around 1 in 2 (50%).[72] Don't focus on the differences, focus on the magnitude of these predictions. If the odds of you dying in a car accident were this high, you would stay home, walk, or ride the bus. The odds of dying in a car crash in the US based on 2021 data was 1 in 93 (1.07%). Wouldn't it be great if we could reduce the future risks of humanity experiencing a major catastrophe to that level?

We should use this type of risk assessment to intelligently determine priorities fitting to the level and certainty of these threats. All these risks are important, but we have limited funds and time, so priorities need to be set. We need to focus on eliminating nuclear weapons, take environmental and climate change risks more seriously, and immediately start considering how to control future risks of genetic engineering and AI. We should not spend billions on sexy projects limiting low risks, such as missile systems for diverting asteroids away from our planet, until the higher priority risks are greatly reduced or eliminated.

In the next section I will attempt to explain why we are not making progress reducing these important threats.

PART THREE

THE MANY EXCUSES WHY WE ARE NOT MAKING PROGRESS

"If the Webers invite us to their vegan potluck dinner, I found an excuse we haven't used yet."

Life is good

"I just want to lie on the beach and eat hot dogs. That's all I've ever wanted."
— Kevin Malone, *The Office.*

For most of us who live in the developed world, life is good. We enjoy comfortable lives relatively safe from immediate threats. We have food, safe drinking water, and enjoy endless diversions that keep us entertained. This makes it hard for us to imagine humanity possibly having a grim future. We may already be aware of risks to humanity, but these risks seem distant and uncertain. Besides, things usually work out for us. Some new technologies will come along to solve all our problems. And experts usually overestimate future risks to humanity. After all, the dire predictions about overpopulation made in the 70s did not come true. Unfortunately, this false sense of security may lead to our downfall. The overpopulation issue remains with us, and its potential impact is amplified by our overreliance on technology to support our increasingly overpopulated planet. Our environment is failing, and we may not even be able to support our current population for much longer.

It is essential that we identify attitudes that hold us back if we are to have any chance to create a safe and sustainable future. One of the most difficult obstructions to overcome is to gain broad public awareness and concern about future risks. This is difficult to achieve for many reasons: 1) These risks do not impact our daily lives; 2) People are flooded with information and it is difficult to break through that noise to get their attention; 3) We tend to have an optimism bias and believe future problems will work themselves out; 4) There is a high level of social and political divisiveness; 5) We are confronted with misinformation that creates doubt about future concerns, such as the campaigns to convince us that climate change is not happening; and 6) Short term thinking—politicians are concerned about issues that impact the next election; business leaders are focused on maximizing profits before the next quarterly stockholders report. The following muses focus on these and other roadblocks to our progress.

Twenty-nine dragons to slay

"Fairy tales are more than true: not because they tell us that dragons exist, but because they tell us that dragons can be beaten."
— Neil Gaiman, *Coraline.*

In his article *The Dragons of Inaction*, psychologist Robert Gifford identified 29 possible roadblocks to achieving progress on environmental issues like climate change.[1] Examples include:

- Perceived inequity: "Why should I change if they won't change?"
- Perceived behavioral control and self-efficacy: When problems are global many individuals believe they can do nothing about them.
- Ignorance: Not knowing that a problem exists or not knowing what to do once one becomes aware of the problem.

- Judgmental discounting: Undervaluing the importance of distant or future issues.
- Environmental numbness: Hearing about an environmental issue too often can lead people to tune out the message.
- Behavioral momentum: Habitual behaviors can be extremely resistant to permanent change, especially across whole societies.
- Conflicting values, goals and aspirations: The aspiration to "get ahead" often means engaging in actions that run counter to the goal of reducing one's environmental impacts—buying a larger house or having a fast fuel-guzzling car.
- Mistrust and denial: When trust is absent, as it sometimes is between citizens and scientists or government officials, resistance in one form or another follows. Mistrust can lead to denial of a problem. This often happens in environments rich with fake news and conspiracy theories.

Do any of these roadblocks sound familiar? Gifford's research suggests that the best way to eliminate these barriers to progress is to achieve a shift in social values. The more altruistic and the less egoistic one's general values are, the more likely one will be concerned about environmental and social issues. However, this research also shows that people will not act if they do not believe that they are able to make a difference. Much more about changing social values is contained in the last section of this book. Meanwhile, sharpen your sword because these dragons are not easily slain.

Alt facts and uncritical thinking

One of the saddest lessons of history is this: If we've been bamboozled long enough, we tend to reject any evidence of the bamboozle. We're no longer interested in finding out the truth. The bamboozle has captured us. It's simply too painful to acknowledge, even to ourselves, that we've been taken. Once you give a charlatan power over you, you almost never get it back.

— Carl Sagan, a quote from his book The Demon-Haunted World.

Bizarro World is a fictional planet appearing in American comic books that was introduced in the early 1960s. It's a cube-shaped planet where everything is weirdly inverted—white is black, and fiction is truth. Fans of *The Seinfeld Show* will remember the "Bizarro Jerry" episode in which Elaine meets a new group of friends who represent inverted types of the normal Seinfeld gang—kind, considerate, curious about the world around them, and good citizens—complete opposites of Jerry, George, Kramer, and Elaine. Elaine's true self eventually returns with a vengeance and she runs back to her narcissistic tribe by the end of the episode.

We are living in Bizarro World, where many people believe that the COVID-19 vaccine implants a microchip inside you; that the tragic Sandy Hook shooting where twenty-three elementary school students were killed was staged by paid actors; and that Democratic Party leaders ran a sex-trafficking ring out of the Comet Ping Pong pizza restaurant in Washington D.C. (known as Pizzagate). And let's not forget about those secret Jewish space lasers causing the California wildfires.

Misinformation is nothing new. In 44 BCE Mark Antony, the great Roman general, was targeted in a major smear campaign.[2] In 1690, the first newspaper published in British colonial America ran a story about the eldest son of Louis XIV plotting to depose the monarch because of a sexual rivalry. "France is in much trouble (and fear) not only with us but also with his Son," because of reports "that the Father used to lie with the Son's wife."[3] Al Gore's book *Assault on Reason* published in 2007 documents the history of attacks on reason, focusing on the increasing assaults during the time around his campaign to become president. Of course, that was nothing compared to what's going on now. After Trump and QAnon, I long for the days when "W" was president and elections were really stolen.[4]

Today's fake news has evolved considerably from its old-fashioned roots in several ways: 1) It spreads faster and with greater influence; 2) It is mostly created by individuals and not traditional news media; 3) Much of it is an intentional deception, often to make money or spread ideological interests; and 4) It is posted, spread, and enhanced by social media, especially posts that become popular.

We cannot make any progress on securing our future if we cannot separate truth from fiction—full stop! It is not that hard to do this using reason, logic, and scientific methods. The California State University Meriam Library developed the CRAAP test for this very purpose that uses the following criteria:[5]

- Currency: If the article is not recent, the claims may no longer be relevant or have been proven wrong.
- Relevance: You must read past the headline and determine the relevancy of the content for your purposes.
- Authority: Does the author have demonstrated expertise and experience? What is the source?
- Accuracy: Can the content be verified by multiple sources? Is it factual? What is the original source of the story? Do you understand the sources' biases?
- Purpose: The intent of a valid news source is to inform. Inaccurate news articles are often written for the sole purpose of provoking anger, fear, excitement, or confirmation of beliefs.

Also, there are guides for determining the bias in traditional news sources. One example can be found on the web at adfontesmedia.com. Sources like AP Reuters, PBS, The New York Times, The Economist, Bloomberg, the Wall Street Journal and The Washington Post are relatively neutral and highly reliable. Other sources like MSNBC, Fox News, Slate, and the New York Post are skewed left or right and are much less reliable in producing original fact reporting.

In the academic world, peer reviews and journal reputation are key indicators of trustworthiness. Journals such as *Science, The New England Journal of Medicine*, and *Nature* rank high. Non-peer-reviewed scientific publications are less reliable. I am not saying that everything published in a peer-reviewed journal is the absolute truth, but it generally represents the best of our current knowledge. Inaccurate publications are quickly torn to shreds in a world where expert peer reviewers guard the publication gate. In fact, it seems to be a popular sport to shoot down your colleagues in the "take no prisoners" academic world that I was a member of for 30 years. A world where truth floats to the top, unlike the toilet bowl world of social media, where much information stinks and sticks to the bottom.

Death by 1000 distractions

"What Orwell feared were those who would ban books. What Huxley feared was that there would be no reason to ban a book, for there would be no one who wanted to read one...Huxley feared we would become a trivial culture, preoccupied with some equivalent of the feelies, the orgy porgy, and the centrifugal bumblepuppy."
— Neil Postman, commenting on Orwell's *1984* and Huxley's *Brave New World* in his book *Amusing Ourselves to Death.*

If you are a baby boomer like me, you were born into a world with very few distractions. Phones were wired to the wall and had a big rotary dial on them. Ours was avocado green. Phone numbers were stored in our heads or were written on a piece of paper pinned on the wall. We had three to four broadcast TV channels to watch, broadcast radio and maybe a record player, if you were lucky. There were no computers, social media, email, video tapes, cable TV, Netflix, CDs, or virtual reality headsets. In fact, the portable cassette tape players did not come out until 1979, when I was already 20 years old. The old joke "All we had to play with was a rock and a can" was not far from the truth. Recalling this makes me feel incredibly old.

Life is very different now—we have more distractions than ever. We have hundreds of cable channels to watch when we are not binge-watching Netflix, Amazon Prime, Apple TV, Hulu.... We communicate through Facebook, Instagram, X, TikTok, LinkedIn… We make love connections through Tinder, Our Time, Grinder… Even an old dude like me is more distracted. As I am trying to write this muse, I hear my neighbor watching soccer on the Sports Channel and my partner is in the next room binge watching Netflix. I am monitoring my email in the background on my laptop, and I have checked WhatsApp on my phone at least five times trying to coordinate a meeting of our beer-drinking "thinktank" group later this week. In about an hour, I need to drop everything to go play pickleball.

Generations Z and Alpha were born into this world of clicking, scrolling, and swiping frantically all day and into the night. They have distractions that most of us boomers can't handle, such as those crazy 3-D fighting video games—I'm a goner within about three seconds. How distracted are we these days? Let's see what some of the research says:[6]

- Apple revealed that iPhones are unlocked an average of 80 times a day.
- 50% say despite their best efforts they sometimes can't stop checking their smartphones when they should be focusing on other things.
- Half the public (49%) say they feel like their attention span is shorter than it used to be, while around a quarter (23%) disagree with this.
- Even more widespread is the belief that young people's attention spans are worse than they were in the past, with two-thirds of people thinking this is the case.
- 47% say that "deep thinking" has become a thing of the past—roughly double the proportion of people who disagree with this view (23%).

This onslaught of distractions is yet another reason why we are not making much progress securing our future. It is difficult to break through this noise. To put this issue in perspective, climate influencer Greta Thunberg has an impressive 14.8M Instagram followers while Kylie Jenner has 294.6M—almost 20 times more. In fact, there are few like Greta among the top 50 Instagram influencers. They are mostly footballers (of the soccer kind), musicians, actresses, and influencers like Kylie showing off their privileged lives. These are the major influences on the generations that are our future. No worries, right?

House of cards

"I remember when I used to go out in Washington, and I'd see Democrats having dinner with Republicans. And they were best friends, and everybody got along. You don't see that too much anymore. In all due respect, you really don't see that. When was the last time you took a Republican out? Why don't you guys go and have dinner together? ...the country is doing well in so many ways, but there's such divisiveness, such division."
— Donald Trump, remarks made during a meeting with bipartisan members of Congress, January 9, 2018.

The series *House of Cards* shows how divisive, backstabbing, self-serving, and narcissistic politicians can be. I personally prefer the original British version shown on the BBC over the more recent US version streamed on Netflix, but both show mind-blowing levels of wickedness.

The sad truth is that *House of Cards* was a preview of the "reality show" politics that we are experiencing today. The US has again become a "house divided against itself."[7] This is not just my opinion. The Eurasiagroup, a thinktank that annually assesses global risks, ranked "The US Against Itself" as the number one risk for 2024. Quoting their report:[8]

"While America's military and economy remain exceptionally strong, its political system is more dysfunctional than that of any other advanced industrial democracy...and in 2024 faces further weakening. The US presidential election will worsen the country's political division, testing American democracy to a degree the nation hasn't experienced in 150 years and undermining US credibility on the global stage."

This divisiveness not only has put us into a political stalemate, but it is also killing our chances to make significant progress on most any issue, including protecting our planet and securing our future. Studies by the Pew Research Center show that divisiveness has tripled over the past four decades. Per surveys done in 2022, 62% of Republicans and 54% of Democrats have a very unfavorable view of the other party, up from 21% and 17% in 1994.[9] This divisiveness keeps us from accomplishing even basic government functions. The US is often on the verge of default these days because politicians cannot agree on an operating budget. If we cannot agree to pay the bills, how will we ever come together to solve the complex issues that lie ahead?

I know it will not be easy, but we need to stop this cultural tug of war and come together in the middle— somewhere in the mud pit where democracy happens. This involves trying to understand the other side and working toward a compromise we all can live with. This means everybody will not get everything they want all the time. Welcome to the real world. Those on the political left need to understand that the cultural change you are pushing always creates friction between new and past ways. Those on the political right need to understand that cultural change happens whether you like it or not.

I remember when I had to listen to a morning prayer in public school and I got paddled when I misbehaved. Much has changed since then, although I must admit that I still misbehave and probably deserve a good paddling. Hopefully someday soon Democrats and Republicans can discuss important issues without attacking each other. We need to live and let live. Then we might have a chance to begin the hard work of saving humanity from itself.

With that said, we cannot let "a confederacy of dunces"[10] limit our development. Think of it as tolerance within reasonable limits. We will never evolve to become a cooperative and sustainable global society if tribalism, misinformation, and short-term thinking wins the day. Hopefully by toning down divisive rhetoric we can start the hard discussions that will get us there.

The church of technology

"Technology is a useful servant but a dangerous master."
— Christian Lous Lange, historian, teacher, and political scientist. Quote from his Nobel Peace Prize lecture given December 13, 1921.

Those that worship the "Church of Technology" believe that it will solve all our problems. It's a belief that no matter how much damage we do, some smart person will invent some new technology that will clean up our mess. Things like the *carbon-matic atmospheric vacuum cleaner* or the *plastic-a-go-go ocean filter*. This is a belief that creates a false sense of security that can make matters much worse.

A more formal term for this belief is the *technocratic paradigm*. A paradigm is a standard, perspective, or set of ideas—a way of looking at something. The term technocratic paradigm was introduced by Pope Frances in his encyclical on the environment called *Laudato Si: On care for our common home.* It's a term used to criticize our tendency to blindly accept and overly depend on technology. Our technocratic paradigm tends to see all of reality as a problem awaiting an application of scientific knowledge and technological power, thus deluding us into thinking we can become powerful enough and wise enough to control all things. We tend to see all of reality as raw material awaiting human use, rather than a living reality, intrinsically valuable and worthy of our respect and protection. This empowers a few elite humans to reduce nature and society to a formless mass awaiting manipulation. Our technocratic paradigm expresses itself economically as wasteful consumerism among the rich, and economic exclusion among the poor. Among the rich, economic interests are best served by simply catering to their every whim, thus maximizing profits and squandering resources. Among the poor, who have few or no economic resources, goods are simply not supplied at all because there is little profit to be made. Our technocratic paradigm tends to concentrate power among those who control financial and political resources, thus encouraging social stratification, creating inequality, and discouraging meaningful change.

A simple way to look at our over-dependence on technology is to compare it to the overuse of credit cards. The more debt you carry, the harder you will fall if something disrupts your incoming cash flow, such as telling your boss to stuff that annual review where the sun doesn't shine.

Technology is not bad in itself. Technology can accomplish much good if used wisely. We must commit to using our intelligence to derive benefits from technology while carefully controlling its negative impacts. We must become better at recognizing the negative impacts of technology. We can no longer allow companies to create technologies reaping massive profits while ignoring destructive impacts. We must hold those making huge profits accountable for damage done. We must have the discipline to limit the development of technologies that clearly cause more harm than good, such as killer robots, engineered plagues, and AI virtual mates. Once a technology is created it is nearly impossible to control, like letting a genie out of its bottle—your wishes will be granted, for better or for worse.

IDEALISTIC PLANS AND REAL PROGRESS

Plan Z

"Saving civilization is not a spectator sport."
— Lester R. Brown, author and eco-warrior.

Over the past 50 years there have been numerous activists that devoted their lives to developing plans to save humanity. Among them, Lester R. Brown is the undisputed champion. Brown is the author or co-author of more than 50 books on environmental issues and saving humanity. One of Brown's last books on this topic was *Plan B 4.0: Mobilizing to Save Civilization* published in 2009. Numerous other activists have enthusiastically pounded their heads against the same wall. Most notable is the Club of Rome research group (Jørgen Randers, Donella Meadows, and others) that collaborated on the 1977 landmark book *The Limits to Growth*, whose research continues today. A few other noteworthy environmental zealots include Aldo Leopold, Paul Ehrlich, James Lovelock, Gus Speth, Paul Hawken, Amory Lovins, David Orr, and William McDonough, to name a few.

Sadly, after over 50 years of dedicated effort producing "Plan Z" and beyond, the needle has not moved much on saving humanity from itself. The problem with these idealistic plans is they do not meet people where they live. We need to have billions on board to make significant progress. As I noted in the previous section of this book, there are many roadblocks that keep the average person from responding. We need to find a way to overcome those barriers.

If aspirational plans from environmental evangelists don't work, what will? If you look at history there are many examples of significant social transformations around issues of concern, such as the abolition of slavery, the Civil Rights Movement, and the green movement of the 60s and 70s. If you look at human development over the long term, we have slowly become more civilized over time. This is painstakingly documented in Steven Pinker's *The Better Angels of Our Nature*. Believe it or not, we now live in a safer and more peaceful world. Pinker analyzes masses of historic data showing that violence has been on a continuous major decline for the past 5,000 years. Rates of all sorts of violence are declining over the long term—murder, torture, and war casualties. We no longer have the stomach for the extreme violence that was common in the Middle Ages. We must admit that public torture and beheadings in the town square are not as popular as they used to be, although they may make a comeback if the current trends in political divisiveness continue to rise.

Let's revisit the social transformations that occurred around the first Earth Day in 1970 as a good model for what works. In the 70s a strong and vocal grass roots movement created significant political pressure that got the attention of congress and the president. Not everyone was on board, but the social and political pressure was great enough to overcome major resistance. This alignment of top-down with bottom-up forces is key to achieve transformational change. Peer pressure works to some extent, but nothing accelerates societal change like the threat of a big fine or jail time. We need grass roots forces to come out in mass protesting in ways that get the attention of the public along with political and corporate leaders—as the hippies and eco-enthusiasts did in the 60s and 70s. We need strong political and corporate leaders to make a stand showing others how to value people and the planet instead of just focusing on political power and profits. People need significant pressure from all sides to motivate billions to change.

Sustainability and other dirty words

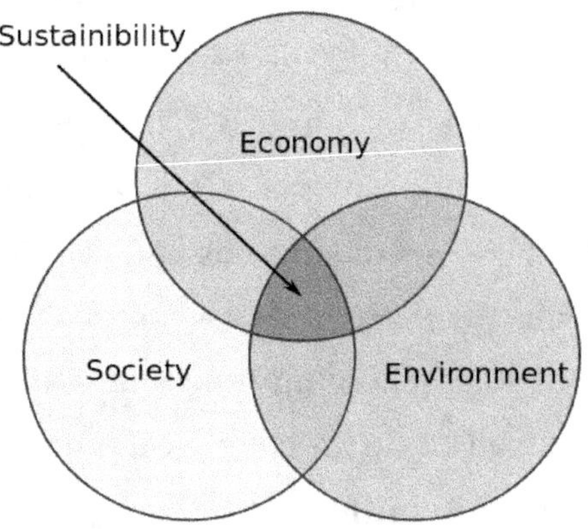

Sustainability Venn diagram[1]

After many years of promoting sustainability, I must confess that it is a concept that is far from perfect. Sustainability is not the same as environmental conservation. Sustainability is a compromise between meeting the needs of people while hopefully not destroying the environment and still making a buck. The three P's – people, planet, and profit. But let's face it, in a capitalistic system, making a profit is priority one. "It's the economy stupid" was coined by James Carville in 1992 when he was advising Bill Clinton in his successful run for the White House. Today, the economy is still at the top of the list of voter concerns going into the 2024 election despite the US enjoying historic job growth.[2] We desperately need to adjust our priorities to achieve a more balanced perspective on what's important. Our good economy won't last if we overly exploit the environment and the people that support it.

The original definition of sustainability was introduced in 1987 by the United Nations Brundtland Commission as "meeting the needs of the present without compromising the ability of future generations to meet their own needs." This is a worthy goal, but it has its difficulties. How do we determine the needs of people living in the future? I'm not sure we can even agree on what our needs are today. Also, it is difficult to make projections into the future, especially projections that go beyond 20 years.

To address these challenges, a new definition of sustainability was developed in 1997 called the "Triple Bottom Line" (TBL).[3] TBL measures social impact, environmental impact, and economic cost—people, planet, and profit. Sustainability is achieved when an idea minimizes negative social and environmental impacts at an acceptable cost. The good thing is that all these factors are measurable and there is no need for complex future projections. The downside is the TBL approach is highly subjective. How much social and environmental damage is acceptable? What is a reasonable cost? Also, an idea may be the best choice using the TBL approach and still not be sustainable over the long run. TBL is not perfect, but it is much better than only considering economics.

One important step in achieving sustainability is to develop specific goals to help us get there. There is no set of goals that everyone will agree with, but there are many values most of us share. The United Nations in 2015 established Sustainable Development Goals (SDGs) to achieve a more equitable and sustainable future for all.[4] The SDGs were ratified by all 193 governments at the United Nations, including the United States. The 17 SDGs are listed below:

1. No poverty.
2. Zero hunger.
3. Good health and well-being.
4. Quality education.
5. Gender equality.
6. Clean water and sanitation.
7. Affordable and clean energy.
8. Decent work and economic growth.
9. Industry, Innovation, and Infrastructure.
10. Reduced inequalities.
11. Sustainable cities and communities.
12. Responsible consumption and production.
13. Climate action.
14. Life below water.

15. Life on land.
16. Peace, justice, and strong institutions.
17. Partnerships for the goals.

Unfortunately, a recent United Nations report notes that we are not as far along as originally hoped toward meeting the SDGs. Although progress is slower than expected, this is a great example of a program successfully setting trans-national societal goals to create a more sustainable world.[5] Hopefully the US can catch up with EU countries and others in achieving these important objectives.

Many companies are working to be more sustainable and to diversify their workforce, efforts that fall under what is called the *environmental, social & governance (ESG)* umbrella. Reading the news lately, ESG might as well be a four-letter word. ESG has become a highly polarizing, politicized term that is receiving significant backlash. Anti-woke rhetoric and policies from the far right are targeting companies promoting ESG practices. Also, there is a wave of anti-ESG legislation aimed at companies that follow ESG principles, causing some companies to downplay or even walk away from their ESG efforts entirely.

Although it's a compromise, sustainability and ESG practices are light years ahead of free-for-all capitalism with few limits exploiting people and trashing the planet for a profit. This is a compromise most businesses and people can live with. Sustainability is a useful tool, and I think we should move forward with it regardless of its faults. It will be good for the planet, people, and business in the long run.

Let's do it like they do it in Finland

Flag of Finland[6]

Which nation is a "shining city on a hill" showing others how to live sustainably? No, Bubba, it's not the USA, it's Finland that leads the world in meeting the United Nations Sustainable Development goals followed closely by Denmark and Sweden.[7] Also, Finland ranks third out of 180 nations in having a low environmental impact per the Yale University Environmental Performance Index.[8] Living sustainably and in harmony with the environment has long been a core Finnish value. The Constitution of the Republic of Finland states that: "Responsibility for the environment Nature and its biodiversity, the environment and the national heritage are the responsibility of everyone. The public authorities shall endeavour to guarantee for everyone the right to a healthy environment and for everyone the possibility to influence the decisions that concern their own living environment."

Not only do the people living in Finland show us good examples of how we can live more sustainably, but they also demonstrate how we can be happier. The World Happiness Reports, published annually since 2012, consistently ranks Finland and other Scandinavian nations high. There is a strong correlation between happiness and places where people care about others and their environment. Taxes are high in Finland, but there is considerable investment in infrastructure, social, and environmental programs to make life better for all while not sacrificing economic viability.

Nations with more of an individualist "sink or swim" approach typically rank lower in happiness, inequity, healthcare, and sustainability. For example, the United States was ranked 15th in the 2023 World Happiness Report. Despite being the richest nation on the planet, the US has one of the highest levels of economic and social inequity amongst developed nations.[9] The US is the only developed nation without a national healthcare program and ranks last among the richest 11th nations for health metrics while healthcare costs more than five times the average of other developed countries.[10] The US ranks 39th in achieving sustainable development goals, just below Belarus. All unfortunate since I believe that most people want to be happy and healthy, and live in an equitable and sustainable society.

I can tell you from personal experience that life is better living in a place that focuses more on personal welfare than piling up wealth and useless stuff. I spent my first 60 years living and working in the US. I decided to retire in 2019. I walked away from a prestigious and well-paying job, sold my expensive home by the beach fully furnished, gathered my clothes and a few keepsakes, and jumped on a plane to Spain. I now live a simpler and more sustainable life in an 850€ per month apartment with an amazing view of the mountains in an idyllic 382-year-old village 10 minutes from the sea. I am happier and healthier than I have ever been. I do not miss all those fine things I left behind. In general, Spaniards are more focused on family, friends, and enjoying life. Their goal is to work enough to live well, not work endlessly to have the most money, the biggest house, and the flashiest car. I am not saying life is perfect. There are too few good job opportunities, especially for young people. But the weather is nice, the cost of living is low, there are decent social programs, and an easy-to-use and effective national health care system.

So, we all should live like Finns, right? Not so fast! If the world became Finlandia we would need over three Earths to support all of us based on their ecological footprint.[11] There is a strong correlation between economic strength and resource consumption. The rule of thumb is "25% of the richest people consume 75% of the world's resources." So, we need to live like Finns' but consume resources like the average Indian (from India, Bubba). A big adjustment for us Americanos to make.

Dr. W.'s dire forecast for humanity

"There are known knowns; there are things we know we know. We also know there are known unknowns; that is to say we know there are some things we do not know. But there are also unknown unknowns—the ones we don't know we don't know."
— Donald Rumsfeld, Secretary of Defense under George W. Bush.

As Donald Rumsfeld says, there are known knowns, known unknowns, and unknown unknowns. Confused? Of course you are. Reality involves much uncertainty, and we must get comfortable with that, especially when pondering our future. Making a long-term forecast for humanity is a tricky business. The best we can do is examine past trends and make an educated guess where we might go from here.

One important thing about doing any type of forecast is choosing what data to include in your analysis. Many trends are getting better. Air quality has improved in the US and many developed countries, and water quality has improved in some areas such as the Chesapeake Bay and the Everglades. Many countries, companies and organizations have started working to become more sustainable and reduce greenhouse gas emissions. We have reduced the total number of nuclear warheads substantially. If you focus on those trends, you will conclude that we have a bright future with no problems. This is a message that all of us would like to hear—no worries, everything will be fine.

I base my forecast on the major indicators of global sustainability. My analysis examines trends in human population, resource supply and use, ecosystem health, biodiversity, and technological threats. Why is my forecast dire? Because all these trends are moving in the wrong direction. Our population has more than doubled in the past 50 years and we are not finished procreating yet, we use more resources per person than ever, so much so that we need almost two Earths to support us, and we have damaged the environment to such an extent that we are starting an extinction event that may rival the past five major ones. Not to mention we are rapidly changing the Earth's climate and we still have enough nukes to plunge us into a mini-ice age that could wipe us out. And now we are creating new technologies including genetic engineering and AI that could be more dangerous than nuclear weapons, with the potential to end civilization as we know it, if they are not carefully controlled.

As I noted in the beginning of this book, we can solve all the problems we are creating. We generally know what we should do, how to do it, and have the resources to do it. But we do not have the social and political will to get it done. Quoting Jean-Claude Juncker, past President of the European Commission: "We all know what to do; we just don't know how to get re-elected after we've done it." We may hope that transformational social and political change will turn things around. But to get billions on board, we would need to become a more altruistic and globally cooperative society. We would need widespread concern about how we impact the environment and threaten our future. We would need to use our intelligence to make decisions based on facts and reason. Misinformation and caustic divisiveness would need to be things of the past.

If you are a Pollyanna optimist who thinks that we are on the cusp of achieving an altruistic globally cooperative society, you would be wrong. Studies indicate that altruism, trust in our institutions, and concern for the environment are declining while divisiveness and misinformation are increasing.[12,13,14,15] These trends are not true for all groups. For example, concern for the environment has recently increased among those under thirty.[16] But on average, these societal trends are going in the wrong direction. One thing that is moving in the right direction is our intelligence has increased by about three IQ points per generation,[17] but we don't seem to have the wisdom to know how to use it. After COVID-19, I did not see people wanting to participate in a reflective movement to better deal with virus-related threats to humanity. What I saw were countless individuals that could not wait to rip off their masks and get back to consuming mass quantities of stuff. Not to mention the enormous amount of misinformation generated during the COVID-19 epidemic.

Let's examine humanity's possible future paths. There are three that cover most near-term possibilities: 1) We avoid future risks and achieve a sustainable global society; 2) We experience a global downfall followed by a recovery; and 3) We experience a global downfall without a recovery. Options one and two could be combined in a variety of ways. For example, you could initially have one or more global downfalls where economies, resources, and populations drop dramatically followed by recoveries where we eventually achieve a sustainable steady state. Alternatively, you could have a period that is safe and sustainable that deteriorates into a downfall with recovery and possibly repeat that cycle a few times. Humanity is done for if option three ever happens.

History teaches us that societies commonly experience major downfalls. The ruins of once great civilizations scattered around the world remind us of this. I am afraid that humanity may need to take a major fall before we become motivated to live cooperatively and sustainably. Based on my risk assessment, I estimate that the odds of us experiencing a global catastrophe over the next century are 1 in 3 or 33%. Of course, this means that we have a 2 in 3 or

67% chance of not living through a global catastrophe. We should not be comfortable with those odds. If you are, then you would be comfortable playing a game of Russian Roulette with two bullets in a six-shot revolver. Sit tight while I go get my pistol…

The alternative happy ending

If you want a happy ending, that depends, of course, on where you stop your story.
— Orson Welles.

I do not want to end this book with a forecast of humanity falling without a possible happy ending. Although I am a big fan of apocalyptic films, I don't want us to experience a real one. There are many examples of transformational change that did not result from a catastrophe. In the late 1700s influential Enlightenment thinkers and Quakers in Britain condemned slavery as morally wrong, which led to the 1833 Abolition of Slavery Act ending this horrible practice in the British Empire without a civil war. In the mid-1800s Susan B. Anthony and Elizabeth Cady Stanton began a movement that eventually resulted in the passage of the Nineteenth Amendment to the United States Constitution giving women the right to vote in 1919. It's not hard to think of other great thinkers and leaders whose ideas and actions had major influence on our world, such as Martin Luther King,

Mahatma Gandhi, John Locke, Adam Smith, and Karl Marx. But transformational social change is never easy and rarely quick.

We need nothing short of a social revolution to get billions of us on board with creating a sustainable and cooperative global society. Social revolutions usually start with cultural change driven by a shift in values and ideals. This can be initiated by a highly influential book, leader, philosophy, new technology, or new idea that spreads rapidly from person to person. Social change is greatly accelerated once the new values and ideals reach politicians and corporate leaders. This can happen in two ways: 1) As the new values spread through society, they also influence political and corporate leaders directly; or 2) When voters and consumers are influenced by new values, they pressure politicians and corporations to adopt the new ideals. A key catalyst for accelerating social change is education, which can be done in schools and through media campaigns. Once new values are adopted by most people, politicians, and the corporate world, then legislation and funding will follow to help fully establish the change.

Social transformations tend to follow an S-curve pattern as shown in the figure below.[18] At the beginning, change slowly increases over time. As an idea gets increasing exposure and popularity, the change rate increases greatly. Nearing the end of the transition, the change rate slows down due to remaining holdouts resisting the trend. Where is the sustainability revolution on the S-curve? The idea was born in the 1990s and is slowly spreading as people, corporations, and nations make efforts to become sustainable. Will the idea spread fast enough to save us from catastrophe? You already know my opinion from the last muse. Hopefully we can accelerate sustainable change to lower our chances of taking a fall.

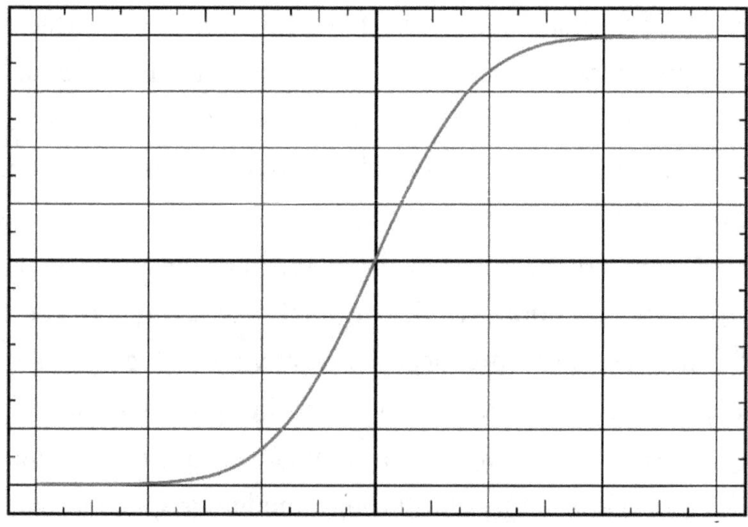

Change adoption S-curve.[19]

We have the knowledge and ability to reduce the risks that threaten our future and to increase our overall wellbeing. This hard work is easier said than done. Quoting one of my comedy heroes Jon Stewart:

> *"The work of making this world resemble one*
> *that you would prefer to live in is a lunch pail*

> *[bleep] job, day in and day out, where thousands of committed, anonymous, smart, and dedicated people bang on closed doors and pick up those who are fallen and grind away on issues until they get a positive result. And even then, have to stay on to make sure that result holds."* [20]

What I present in the following paragraphs is the structural framework that could help support the transformational change needed for us not only to survive, but to thrive. This is based on a talk I gave called *Developing a Sustainable Vision for the US.*[21]

<u>We must be smart</u>

We need to use our best intelligence to have a chance at a bright future. This requires a commitment to facts, reason, and logic. We must have respect for scientific methods and established experts. We must understand that sources of information matter, that facts may change as our knowledge advances, and that facts are subject to reasonable debate. If we want to advance, there is no room for "alternative" facts based on unreliable sources.

The need for us to be smart is the most important factor to achieve a safe and sustainable future. Researchers with the Club of Rome collaborative have used complex computer models to study the future of humanity for over 50 years. Their computer model *Earth 3* simulates global economic, social, and environmental systems to determine if a course of future action is sustainable. Their projections show that if we keep doing the same without transformational change humanity will experience a major fall. Their results also show that solely relying on technology will not save us, nor will working harder. They show that living smarter gives humanity the best chance of living well and avoiding a fall.[22]

We must be fair

We must make decisions that are in everyone's best interest, for people living now and those that will live in the future. Beyond this being the right thing to do, history teaches us that people that are downtrodden and abused too long will revolt against their oppressors.

Being fair includes applying the principles of fair wages and taxation, achieving reasonable equity while not taking away incentives for business development. Fairness should result in an eventual leveling of the economic playing field within nations and globally. Finding the right balance between business incentive and taxation of wealth is not only fair, but it also creates a stronger overall economy by keeping more funds in circulation. The goal is not to create a world of selfless individuals with no ambition, but to create societies that value balancing self-interests with what is best for our local, national, and global societies. We need the freedom and incentive to achieve business and personal success, but we must have the resolve to set firm limits on the negative impacts these "successes" have on others and on our planet.

We must protect the environment and conserve natural resources

Earth provides us with the life support systems we need to survive—air, water, food, and many other resources. We have done much damage to these support systems. We must take a stronger stand against further damage. Approval of projects and products that damage the planet should be the exception and not the rule. And any damage done needs to be carefully thought through and successfully mitigated. With eight billion of us on board, we need to act cautiously to keep the planet healthy and our life support systems operating. Also, we need to slow down the genocide of species that share the Earth with us. Not only is it the right thing to do, but we also derive many benefits from these species and the complex web of life they support.

We must invest in our future

We must invest financially in our future to achieve the best outcome for younger and future generations. Financial support of education, research, and infrastructure can go a long way to creating a brighter future for everyone. Funding is essential to making change happen, especially when dealing with complex global issues. When cultural changes impact political realms then budgets will be redistributed to meet the new societal goals. Nations with cooperative cultures that seek the common good for all citizens tend to have higher taxes for the wealthy and use those funds to support health, education, and common infrastructure needs of all citizens.

We must cooperate globally

Whether you like it or not, we are part of an interconnected global society. Problems in one place can impact all of us. Two recent examples of this are COVID-19 and the Great Recession of 2008-2009. It is increasingly important that we achieve global cooperation among all nations as we develop dangerous new technologies such as artificial intelligence and genetic engineering. Even one uncooperative nation could become a haven for those that seek to do humanity harm.

We need a global government or some universally accepted institutions where national leaders can discuss issues and develop agreements to manage these risks. Perhaps a revised United Nations that has "teeth" to enforce agreements could meet this need. Beyond managing threats to humanity like artificial intelligence and nuclear weapons, effective global cooperation could help solve numerous issues, such as ending war, extreme poverty, and famine.

Another benefit of global cooperation is there would be less need for individual nations to have large military budgets. The US spends 55% of its total budget on the military, more than five times the per capita spent by any other nation. The US accounts for 39% of world military spending, three times more than China and ten times more than Russia.[23] In a world of cooperative peace agreement with global enforcement, this large sum of money could be used to help solve many other national and global issues.

<u>We must reduce or eliminate the risks that we are creating</u>

We must immediately start working to lower the risks resulting from the problems that we have caused. Here are a few ideas that may help to reduce these risks—equivalent of a "speed dating" session to solve all the world's problems. Again, these are easier said than done. But all are solvable once we have the social and political will to get off the couch and on with it.

- **Overpopulation:** Work to enhance economic development in less developed nations; provide birth control education and resources; educate and empower women.
- **Resource consumption:** Discourage excessive consumption; regulate wasteful products and processes; find alternative sustainable resources; encourage reuse, recycling, and repurposing.

- **Environmental damage:** Set stronger limits on ecological damage; incentivize restoration efforts; develop compact walkable/bikeable cities while limiting further greenspace development; incentivize sustainable agricultural practices; greatly reduce environmental toxification; increase areas of protected natural habitats.
- **Climate change:** Establish tax and regulatory incentives to speed the transition to renewables; end subsidies to nonrenewable energy; encourage energy efficiency and wise use.
- **Miscellaneous risks:** Evaluate and monitor risks; establish and maintain regulations that protect global economic stability; establish effective global cooperation and governance mechanisms.
- **Nuclear weapons:** Enforce the UN treaty banning nuclear weapons and establish effective mechanisms for cooperation, inspection, and enforcement.
- **Genetic engineering and AI:** Create strong and cooperative global regulatory programs to limit development of dangerous genetic engineering and AI practices. Establish necessary regulations and monitoring systems to discourage malicious use of these technologies. Work to resolve the ethical and psychological issues driving some people to want to harm others.

<u>We must develop a common global vision for our future</u>

Once we have successfully managed future risks, we can take time for a period of reflection to develop a shared vision and goals for the future of our global community. These goals can become a foundation for global governance and cooperation, such as a global constitution. Of course, there is no set of goals that everyone will agree with, but there are many values most of us share. The United Nations Sustainable Development Goals is a great place to start.

This was just a short summary of a few ideas that could help us move toward a safe and sustainable future. There is simply not enough space in this short muse to do justice to this important topic. Besides, I need something to write about for my next book.

I will finish by revisiting a central question of this book: "Will our intelligence save us or destroy us?" The answer depends on what we do and how fast we do it. If we continue to live for short term gains while giving too little attention toward future risks, then we expose ourselves to significant threats that could possibly end humanity. If we start living more intelligently and cooperatively, we will greatly improve our chances to avoid catastrophe and to thrive. It is our choice—I hope that we choose to use our intelligence to create a safer and sustainable society that protects our planet and serves the best interests of all who live in our global village.

Notes

PART ONE

[1] Schmidt, Ingrid. 2024. "Billionaires' Survivalist Bunkers Go Absolutely Bonkers with Fiery Moats and Water Cannons." *The Hollywood Reporter,* February 12, 2024. https://www.hollywoodreporter.com/lifestyle/lifestyle-news/bunkers-billionaires-survive-apocalypse-cost-features-1235822762/

[2] The Anthropocene is becoming a commonly used term, but it is not yet officially recognized as a unit within the Geological Time Scale. The Anthropocene Working Group in the International Commission on Stratigraphy is charged with the task of gathering data to make this designation official. More information can be found at http://quaternary.stratigraphy.org/working-groups/anthropocene/.

[3] Dates and details about prehistoric human development are constantly evolving as more fossil and genetic evidence is found. New evidence shows our history is older than previously thought. Current timelines and information can be found at the Smithsonian Human Origins Initiative website: https://humanorigins.si.edu/.

[4] Smithsonian Human Origins Initiative. n.d. "Ancient DNA and Neanderthals." Accessed August 3, 2023. https://humanorigins.si.edu/evidence/genetics/ancient-dna-and-neanderthals

[5] Raff, Jennifer. 2021. "Genomes Reveal Humanity's Journey into the Americas." *Scientific American,* May 1, 2021. https://www.scientificamerican.com/article/genomes-reveal-humanitys-journey-into-the-americas/.

[6] Switek, Brian. 2011. "Mastodon Fossil Throws Up Questions Over 'Rapid' Extinction." *Nature*, October 20,

2011. https://doi.org/10.1038/news.2011.606.

[7] Carey, John. 2023. "Unearthing the Origins of Agriculture." *Proceedings of the National Academy of Sciences*, 120 (15) https://doi.org/10.1073/pnas.2304407120.

[8] All early population estimates taken from summaries of research data posted by the United States Census Bureau. 2022. "Historical Estimates of World Population." Last modified December 5, 2022. https://www.census.gov/data/tables/time-series/demo/international-programs/historical-est-worldpop.html.

[9] British Library. n.d. "Where did Writing Begin?" Accessed July 28, 2023. https://www.bl.uk/history-of-writing/articles/where-did-writing-begin.

[10] World History Encyclopedia. 2020. "The Printing Revolution in Renaissance Europe." Accessed July 28, 2023. https://www.worldhistory.org/article/1632/the-printing-revolution-in-renaissance-europe/.

[11] Encyclopædia Britannica. 2023. "The first Industrial Revolution." Accessed July 28, 2023. https://www.britannica.com/money/topic/Industrial-Revolution/.

[12] Hanlon, Walker. 2015. "Pollution and Mortality in the 19th Century." Working Paper 21647, National Bureau of Economic Research, Published October 2015. https://www.nber.org/system/files/working_papers/w21647/w21647.pdf.

[13] McVean, Ada. 2020. "An Environmental Disaster Brought to You by Meat: Chicago's Bubbly Creek." *Skeptical Inquirer Magazine,* March 27, 2020. https://skepticalinquirer.org/exclusive/an-environmental-disaster-brought-to-you-by-meat-chicagos-bubbly-creek/.

[14] Drucker, Peter. 1999. "Beyond the Information Revolution." *The Atlantic*, October 1999. https://www.theatlantic.com/magazine/archive/1999/10/b

eyond-the-information-revolution/304658/.

[15] American Physical Society. 2007. "December 1938: Discovery of Nuclear Fission." Posted December 2007. https://www.aps.org/publications/apsnews/200712/physicshistory.cfm.

[16] Wells, Steve. 2013. *Drunk with Blood: God's Killings in the Bible.* SAB Books. ISBN-10: 0988245116.

[17] Persaud, Raj and Peter Bruggen. 2015. "Why Some People Think the Apocalypse Is Coming Soon." *Psychology Today,* September 12, 2015. https://www.psychologytoday.com/us/blog/slightly-blighty/201509/why-some-people-think-the-apocalypse-is-coming-soon.

[18] Bulkeley, Kelly. 2022. "Why People Dream of Apocalypse." *Psychology Today,* January 5, 2022. https://www.psychologytoday.com/us/blog/dreaming-in-the-digital-age/202201/why-people-dream-apocalypse.

[19] Csikszentimihalyi, Mihaly. 1990. *Flow: The Psychology of Optimal Experience.* New York: Harper & Row. ISBN-10: 0061339202.

[20] American Psychological Association. n.d. "APA Dictionary of Psychology." Accessed July 29, 2023. https://dictionary.apa.org/self-fulfilling-prophecy.

[21] In the book *Airs, Waters, and Places,* thought to have been written by Greek physician Hippocrates in the 5th or 4th century BCE, the first systematic attempt was made to set forth a causal relationship between human diseases and environmental pollution.

[22] National Museum of Nuclear Science and History. n.d. "Russell-Einstein Manifesto." Accessed July 29, 2023. https://ahf.nuclearmuseum.org/ahf/key-documents/russell-einstein-manifesto/.

[23] BirdLife International. 2022. "State of the World's Birds 2022." Posted September 27, 2022. https://www.birdlife.org/papers-reports/state-of-the-

worlds-birds-2022/

[24] BBC. 2023. "How the Largest Environmental Movement in History was Born." Posted April 23, 2023. https://www.bbc.com/future/article/20200420-earth-day-2020-how-an-environmental-movement-was-born.

[25] YouTube. n.d. Scene from 1991 movie *Terminator 2: Judgment Day.* Accessed July 29, 2023. https://www.youtube.com/watch?v=kahHJLfVP84.

[26] YouTube. n.d. Scene from the 1992 movie *A Few Good Men.* Accessed July 29, 2023. https://www.youtube.com/watch?v=9FnO3igOkOk.

PART TWO

[1] National Safety Council. n.d. "Lifetime odds of death for selected causes, United States, 2021." Accessed November 29, 2023. https://injuryfacts.nsc.org/all-injuries/preventable-death-overview/odds-of-dying/

[2] Bostrom, Nick. 2013. "Existential Risk Prevention as Global Priority" *Global Policy,* February 2013. https://onlinelibrary.wiley.com/doi/abs/10.1111/1758-5899.12002.

[3] Urban, Tim. 2013. "7.3 billion people, one building." Waitbutwhy.com, posted March 3, 2015. Used with permission. https://waitbutwhy.com/2015/03/7-3-billion-people-one-building.html.

[4] United Nations. n.d. "World population to reach 8 billion on 15 November 2022." Accessed November 29, 2023. https://www.un.org/en/desa/world-population-reach-8-billion-15-november-2022.

[5] United Nations Environmental Program. 2012. "One Planet, How Many People? A Review of Earth's Carrying Capacity." Posted June 6, 2012. https://wedocs.unep.org/handle/20.500.11822/40937.

[6] Ritchie, Hannah, Lucas Rodés-Guirao, Edouard Mathieu,

Marcel Gerber, Esteban Ortiz-Ospina, Joe Hasell, and Max Roser. 2023. "Population Growth". Accessed November 29, 2023. https://ourworldindata.org/population-growth.

[7] United Nations. n.d. "Global Issues—Population." Accessed November 30, 2023. https://www.un.org/en/global-issues/population.

[8] United Nations. n.d. "World population projected to reach 9.8 billion in 2050, and 11.2 billion in 2100." Accessed November 30, 2023. https://www.un.org/en/desa/world-population-projected-reach-98-billion-2050-and-112-billion-2100.

[9] Quiverfull. n.d. Accessed November 30, 2023. https://www.quiverfull.com/.

[10] United Nations. 2022. "World Population Prospects 2022." Accessed November 30, 2023. https://desapublications.un.org/file/989/download.

[11] World Food Programme. n.d. "World Hunger Map." Accessed November 30, 2023. https://hungermap.wfp.org/.

[12] Bongaarts, John and Dennis Hodgson. 2022. "The Impact of Voluntary Family Planning Programs on Contraceptive Use, Fertility, and Population." In: *Fertility Transition in the Developing World*. SpringerBriefs in Population Studies. Springer, Cham. https://doi.org/10.1007/978-3-031-11840-1_7.

[13] NASA. 2006. "The Earth seen from Apollo 17." Wikimedia Commons, posted March 6, 2006. https://en.wikipedia.org/wiki/The_Blue_Marble.

[14] Shaw, Lucas. 2020. "These Are Netflix's 10 Most Popular Original Movies." Bloomberg, accessed February 1, 2024. https://www.bloomberg.com/news/articles/2020-07-15/netflix-most-popular-original-movies?.

[15] Global Footprint Network. n.d. Accessed November 30, 2023. https://www.footprintnetwork.org/.

[16] Global Footprint Network. 2021. "We do not need a pandemic to #MoveTheDate, International organizations agree." Posted January 19, 2021. https://www.footprintnetwork.org/2021/01/19/we-do-not-need-a-pandemic-to-movethedate/.

[17] Bradshaw, Corey J. A., Paul R. Ehrlich, Andrew Beattie, Gerardo Ceballos, Eileen Crist, Joan Diamond, Rodolfo Dirzo, Anne H. Ehrlich, John Harte, Mary Ellen Hart, Graham Pyke, Peter H. Raven, William J. Ripple, Frédérik Saltré, Christine Turnbull, Mathis Wackernagel, and Daniel T. Blumstein. 2021. "Underestimating the Challenges of Avoiding a Ghastly Future." *Front. Conserv. Sci.,* January 13, 2021. https://doi.org/10.3389/fcosc.2020.615419.

[18] Livi-Bacci, Massimo. 2017. *Our Shrinking Planet.* New York: Wiley. ISBN: 978-1-509-51583-7. https://www.wiley.com/en-dk/Our+Shrinking+Planet-p-9781509515844.

[19] Ritchie, Hannah and Pablo Rosado. 2017. "Fossil Fuels" Posted October 2, 2022. https://ourworldindata.org/fossil-fuels'.

[20] International Energy Agency. 2021. "Global Energy Review 2021." IEA, Paris, April 2021. https://www.iea.org/reports/global-energy-review-2021.

[21] International Energy Agency. 2021. "The Role of Critical Minerals in Clean Energy Transitions." IEA, Paris, May 2021. https://www.iea.org/reports/the-role-of-critical-minerals-in-clean-energy-transitions.

[22] U.S. Geological Survey. 2023. "Mineral Commodity Summaries 2023." Posted January 31, 2023. https://doi.org/10.3133/mcs2023.

[23] Davidsson Kurland, Simon, and Sally M. Benson. 2019. "The Energetic Implications of Introducing Lithium-ion Batteries into Distributed Photovoltaic Systems." *Sustainable Energy Fuels,* 3: 1182-1190.

http://dx.doi.org/10.1039/C9SE00127A.

24 Kubiszewski, Ida, Cutler J. Cleveland, and Peter K. Endres. 2010. "Meta-analysis of Net Energy Return for Wind Power Systems." *Renewable Energy,* 35 (1): 218-225. https://www.sciencedirect.com/science/article/abs/pii/S096014810900055X

25 Tang, Didi, Eric Tucker, and Frank Bajak. 2024. "US says it disrupted a China cyber threat but warns hackers could still wreak havoc for Americans." *Associated Press,* February 1, 2024. https://apnews.com/article/fbi-china-espionage-hacking-db23dd96cfd825e4988852a34a99d4ea.

26 Ritchie, Hannah, Pablo Rosado, and Max Roser. 2023. "Hunger and Undernourishment." Published online at OurWorldInData.org. Accessed December 12, 2023. https://ourworldindata.org/hunger-and-undernourishment.

27 Ritchie, Hannah, Pablo Rosado, and Max Roser. 2023. "Agricultural Production." Published online at OurWorldInData.org. Accessed December 12, 2023. https://ourworldindata.org/agricultural-production.

28 U.S. Food and Drug Administration. n.d. "GMO Crops, Animal Food, and Beyond." Accessed December 12, 2023. https://www.fda.gov/food/agricultural-biotechnology/gmo-crops-animal-food-and-beyond.

29 Ryan. 2012. "Food signage at the Canadian National Exhibition, Toronto." Wikimedia Commons. Posted August 29, 2012. https://en.wikipedia.org/wiki/Deep-fried_butter.

30 USDA. n.d. "Food and Nutrition Security." Retrieved December 13, 2023. https://www.usda.gov/nutrition-security%costs%20and%20decreased%20productivity.

31 Ritchie, Hannah. 2020. "You Want to Reduce the Carbon Footprint of Your Food?" Published online at

OurWorldInData.org. Retrieved December 13, 2023. https://ourworldindata.org/food-choice-vs-eating-local.

[32] Muntaka Chasant. 2018. "Plastic Pollution covering Accra beach." Wikimedia Commons. Uploaded October 3, 2018. https://commons.wikimedia.org/wiki/File:Plastic_Polluti on_in_Ghana.jpg.

[33] YouTube. n.d. "Graduate Scene: Plastics." Accessed December 13, 2023. https://www.youtube.com/watch?v=eMtLdE5Zq-8.

[34] National Oceanic and Atmospheric Administration. n.d. "A Guide to Plastic in the Ocean." Accessed December 13, 2023. https://oceanservice.noaa.gov/hazards/marinedebris/plast ics-in-the-ocean.html.

[35] World Economic Forum, Ellen MacArthur Foundation, and McKinsey & Company. 2016. "The New Plastics Economy: Rethinking the future of plastics." https://www.ellenmacarthurfoundation.org/the-new-plastics-economy-rethinking-the-future-of-plastics.

[36] Parker, Laura. 2022. "Microplastics are in our bodies. How much do they harm us?" *National Geographic*, April 26, 2022. https://www.nationalgeographic.co.uk/environment-and-conservation/2022/04/microplastics-are-in-our-bodies-how-much-do-they-harm-us.

[37] Stelle, Laurelle. 2024. "New Study Traces 'Forever Chemicals' to Unexpected Location…" *The Cool Down*, January 17, 2024. https://www.thecooldown.com/green-tech/pfas-pollution-ocean-contamination/.

[38] National Institute of Environmental Sciences. n.d. "Endocrine Disruptors." Accessed February 16, 2024. https://www.niehs.nih.gov/health/topics/agents/endocrine

[39] Rattan, Saniya, Changqing Zhou, Catheryne Chiang, Sharada Mahalingam, Emily Brehm and Jodi Flaws.

2017. "Exposure to endocrine disruptors during adulthood: consequences for female fertility." *The Journal of endocrinology* vol. 233,3: R109-R129. https://joe.bioscientifica.com/view/journals/joe/233/3/R109.xml.

[40] Oystercard. 2023. "Street art mural featuring Greta Thunberg in Istanbul-Kadıköy, Türkiye." Wikimedia Commons, posted January 31, 2023. https://commons.wikimedia.org/wiki/File:Street_art_mural_featuring_Greta_Thunberg_in_Istanbul-Kad%C4%B1k%C3%B6y,_T%C3%BCrkiye.jpg.

[41] National Aeronautics and Space Administration. n.d. "How Do We Know Climate Change Is Real?" Accessed December 13, 2023. https://climate.nasa.gov/evidence/.

[42] National Oceanic and Atmospheric Administration. 2024. "2023 was the world's warmest year on record, by far." Posted January 12, 2024. https://www.noaa.gov/news/2023-was-worlds-warmest-year-on-record-by- far#: ~.

[43] Intergovernmental Panel on Climate Change. 2023. "AR6 Synthesis Report: Climate Change 2023." Accessed December 13, 2023. https://www.ipcc.ch/report/sixth-assessment-report-cycle/.

[44] Steffen, Will, Johan Rockström, and Katherine Richardson. 2018. "Trajectories of the Earth System in the Anthropocene." *Proceedings of the National Academy of Sciences,* 115 (33): 8252–8259. https://www.pnas.org/doi/suppl/10.1073/pnas.1810141115.

[45] Schechinger, Anne. 2020. "The High Cost of Algae Blooms in U.S. Waters." Environmental Working Group, posted August 26, 2020. https://www.ewg.org/research/high-cost-of-algae-blooms.

[46] Black, Simon, Ian Parry, Nate Vernon. 2023. "Fossil Fuel

Subsidies Surged to Record $7 Trillion." IMF Blog, August 24, 2023. https://www.imf.org/en/Blogs/Articles/2023/08/24/fossil-fuel-subsidies-surged-to-record-7-trillion.

[47] United States Department of Energy (https://catalog.archives.gov/id/558579). 2017. "J. Robert Oppenheimer." Wikimedia Commons, posted August 3, 2023. https://en.wikipedia.org/wiki/File:Oppenheimer_(cropped).jpg.

[48] Temperton, James. 2023. "'Now I Am Become Death, the Destroyer of Worlds.' The Story of Oppenheimer's Infamous Quote." *Wired,* July 21, 2023. https://www.wired.co.uk/article/manhattan-project-robert-oppenheimer.

[49] Witmer, Sarah. 2017. Nuclear Close Calls." Waging Peace, posted August 31, 2017, https://www.wagingpeace.org/nuclear-close-calls/.

[50] Federation of American Scientists. 2023. "Status of World Nuclear Forces." Posted March 31, 2023. https://fas.org/initiative/status-world-nuclear-forces/.

[51] Xia, Lin., Alan Robock, Kim Scherrer, Cheryl S. Harrison, Benjamin Leon Bodirsky, Isabelle Weindl, Jonas Jägermeyr, Charles G. Bardeen, Owen B. Toon and Ryan Heneghan. 2022. "Global food insecurity and famine from reduced crop, marine fishery and livestock production due to climate disruption from nuclear war soot injection." *Nature Food,* 3, 586–596. https://doi.org/10.1038/s43016-022-00573-0.

[52] Solodovnikov, Alexey, and Valeria Arkhipova. 2021. "Scientifically accurate atomic model of the external structure of the Severe Acute Respiratory Syndrome CoronaVirus 2 (SARS-CoV-2), a strain (genetic variant) of the coronavirus that caused coronavirus disease (COVID-19), first identified in Wuhan, China, during

December 2019." Wikimedia Commons, posted May 5, 2021. https://commons.wikimedia.org/wiki/File:Coronavirus._SARS-CoV-2.png.

53 Anthony, Andrew. 2017. "Yuval Noah Harari: 'Homo sapiens as we know them will disappear in a century or so." *The Guardian,* March 17, 2017. https://www.theguardian.com/culture/2017/mar/19/yuval-harari-sapiens-readers-questions-lucy-prebble-arianna-huffington-future-of-humanity.

54 Synthego.com. n.d. "History of Genetic Engineering and the Rise of Genome Editing Tools." Accessed December 14, 2023. https://www.synthego.com/learn/genome-engineering-history.

55 Enserink, Martin. 2011. "Scientists Brace for Media Storm Around Controversial Flu Studies." *Science,* November 23, 2011. https://www.science.org/content/article/scientists-brace-media-storm-around-controversial-flu-studies?.

56 Young, Alison. 2023. "Dangerous lab leaks happen far more often than the public is aware." *The Guardian,* May 30, 2023. https://www.theguardian.com/commentisfree/2023/may/30/lab-leaks-shrouded-secrecy.

57 Ray Brown, Timothy. "I Am the Berlin Patient: A Personal Reflection." *AIDS Research and Human Retroviruses,* January 1; 31(1): 2–3. https://doi.org/10.1089/aid.2014.0224.

58 Gallagher, James. 2015. Designer cells' reverse one-year-old's cancer." BBC, posted November 5, 2015. https://www.bbc.com/news/health-34731498.

59 Rees, Martin. 2011. "The world in 2050 and beyond." *The Statesman,* November 26, 2014. https://www.newstatesman.com/long-reads/2014/11/martin-rees-world-2050-and-beyond.

[60] YouTube. n.d. "Monty Python and the Holy Grail: Bring Out Your Dead." Accessed December 15, 2023. https://www.youtube.com/watch?v=x6Ul0thfc_Q.

[61] Kemp, Luke, Laura Adam, Christian Boehm, Rainer Breitling, Rocco Casagrande, Malcolm Dando, Appolinaire Djikeng, Nicholas Evans, Richard Hammond, Kelly Hills, Lauren Holt, Todd Kuiken, Alemka Markotić, Piers Millett, Johnathan Napier, Cassidy Nelson, Seán ÓhÉigeartaigh, Anne Osbourn, Megan Palmer, Nicola Patron, Edward Perello, Wibool Piyawattanametha, Vanessa Restrepo-Schild, Clarissa Rios-Rojas, Catherine Rhodes, Anna Roessing, Deborah Scott, Philip Shapira, Christopher Simuntala, Robert Smith, Lalitha Sundaram, Eriko Takano, Gwyn Uttmark, Bonnie Wintle, Nadia Zahra, and William Sutherland. 2020. "Bioengineering horizon scan 2020." *eLife,* 9: e54489. DOI: https://doi.org/10.7554/eLife.54489.

[62] Schlesener, Ralf. 2019. Campaign to stop killer robots, Berlin visual stunt March 2019. https://www.flickr.com/photos/stopkillerrobots/40467934923/in/album-72157705970474001/.

[63] Cellan-Jones, Rory. 2014. "Stephen Hawking warns artificial intelligence could end mankind." BBC, December 2, 2014. https://www.bbc.com/news/technology-30290540.

[64] Deepmind.com. n.d. "AlphaGo." Accessed December 15, 2023. https://deepmind.google/technologies/alphago/.

[65] Brundage, Miles, Shahar Avin, Jack Clark, Helen Toner, Peter Eckersley, Ben Garfinkel, Allan Dafoe, Paul Scharre, Thomas Zeitzoff, Bobby Filar, Hyrum Anderson, Heather Roff, Gregory Allen, Jacob Steinhardt, Carrick Flynn, Seán ÓhÉigeartaigh, Simon Beard, Haydn Belfield, Sebastian Farquhar, Clare Lyle, Rebecca Crootof, Owain Evans, Michael Page, Joanna Bryson, Roman Yampolskiy, and Dario Amodei. 2018.

"The Malicious Use of Artificial Intelligence: Forecasting, Prevention, and Mitigation." Accessed December 15, 2023. https://maliciousaireport.com/.

[66] Sample, Ian. 2016. "AI will create 'useless class' of human, predicts bestselling historian." *The Guardian,* May 20, 2016. https://www.theguardian.com/technology/2016/may/20/silicon-assassins-condemn-humans-life-useless-artificial-intelligence.

[67] Bostrom, Nick. 2019. "The Vulnerable World Hypothesis." *Global Policy,* 10 (4): 455-476. https://doi.org/10.1111/1758-5899.12718.

[68] Nationaal Archief (https://www.flickr.com/people/29998366@N02). 2016. "A line of unemployed people in Amsterdam, 1933." Wikimedia Commons, posted November 27, 2016. https://commons.wikimedia.org/wiki/File:Werklozen_in_de_rij_-_Row_of_unemployed_(5371990267).jpg.

[69] World Economic Forum. 2021. "The Global Risks Report 2021." WEF, posted January 19, 2021. https://www.weforum.org/publications/the-global-risks-report-2021/.

[70] Ord, Toby. 2020. *The Precipice: Existential Risk and the Future of Humanity.* New York: Hachette Book Group. ISBN-10: 0316484911.

[71] I assume a 10-fold relationship for the killing 25% vs. 100% of our global population because population death studies show this relationship is not linear—it is much harder to kill all a population vs. a fraction of a population. Examples of this research showing this relationship disinfection studies of bacterial populations and risk assessments of meteor size and strike frequency vs. expected human population loss.

[72] Hattenstone, Simon. 2003. "The end of the world as we know it (maybe)." *The Guardian,* April 24, 2003.

https://www.theguardian.com/education/2003/apr/24/research.highereducation.

PART THREE

[1] Gifford, Robert. 2011. "The Dragons of Inaction: Psychological Barriers That Limit Climate Change Mitigation and Adaptation." *American Psychologist,* 66(4): 290-302. https://doi.org/10.1037/a0023566.
[2] Posetti, Julie and Alice Matthews. 2018. "A short guide to the history of 'fake news' and disinformation." International Journalists' Network, posted July 7, 2018. https://www.icfj.org/news/short-guide-history-fake-news-and-disinformation-new-icfj-learning-module.
[3] Yeoman, Barry. 2022. "That's Fake News!" *The Saturday Evening Post,* July 6, 2022. https://www.saturdayeveningpost.com/2022/07/thats-fake-news/.
[4] Chait, Jonathan. 2012. "Yes, Bush v. Gore Did Steal the Election." *New York Magazine,* June 25, 2012. https://nymag.com/intelligencer/2012/06/yes-bush-v-gore-did-steal-the-election.html.
[5] California State University, Chico. 2010. "Evaluating Information – Applying the CRAAP Test." Posted September 17, 2010. https://library.csuchico.edu/sites/default/files/craap-test.pdf.
[6] Kings College London. 2022. "Are attention spans really collapsing?" Posted February 22, 2022. https://www.kcl.ac.uk/news/are-attention-spans-really-collapsing-data-shows-uk-public-are-worried-but-also-see-benefits-from-technology).
[7] National Park Service. n.d. "On June 16, 1858, Lincoln accepted the Republican nomination to run against Douglas and delivered his famous 'House Divided

Speech' in the Illinois state house." Accessed January 18, 2024. https://www.nps.gov/features/liho/life/33.htm.

8 Eurasiagroup. 2024. "Top Risks 2024." Accessed January 18, 2024. https://www.eurasiagroup.net/issues/top-risks-2024.

9 Pew Research Center. 2022. "As Partisan Hostility Grows, Signs of Frustration with the Two-Party System." Posted August 9, 2022. https://www.pewresearch.org/politics/2022/08/09/as-partisan-hostility-grows-signs-of-frustration-with-the-two-party-system/.

10 Referring to the book *A Confederacy of Dunces* by John Kennedy Toole.

PART FOUR

1 Nicoguaro. 2023. "Sustainability Venn Diagram." Wikimedia Commons. Posted June 21, 2023. https://commons.wikimedia.org/wiki/File:Sustainability_venn_diagram.svg.

2 Oshin, Olafimihan. 2023. "Most voters under 30 say economy is biggest issue as 2024 nears." *The Hill,* December 9, 2023. https://thehill.com/homenews/campaign/4351561-voters-under-30-economy-biggest-issue-2024-poll/.

3 Elkington, John. 1997. *Cannibals with Forks: The Triple Bottom Line of 21st Century.* Wiley: New York.

4 United Nations. n.d. "The 17 Goals." Accessed December 19, 2023. https://sdgs.un.org/goals.

5 United Nations. 2023. "World risks big misses across the Sustainable Development Goals unless measures to accelerate implementation are taken, UN warns." Posted July 10, 2023. https://www.un.org/en/desa/world-risks-big-misses-across-sustainable-development-goals-unless-

measures-accelerate.

[6]Santeri Viinamäki, 2018. "Flag of Finland." Wikimedia Commons. Posted December 6, 2018. https://en.wikipedia.org/wiki/Flag_of_Finland.

[7] Sustainable Development Report. n.d. "Rankings." Accessed December 19, 2023. https://dashboards.sdgindex.org/rankings.

[8] Environmental Performance Index. n.d. "2022 Results." Yale University, accessed December 19, 2023. https://epi.yale.edu/epi-results/2022/component/epi.

[9] Schaeffer, Katherine. 2020. "6 facts about economic inequality in the U.S." Pew Research Center, posted February 7, 2020. https://www.pewresearch.org/short-reads/2020/02/07/6-facts-about-economic-inequality-in-the-u-s/.

[10] Parker, Claire. 2021. "U.S. health-care system ranks last among 11 high-income countries, researchers say." *The Washington Post,* August 5, 2021. https://www.washingtonpost.com/world/2021/08/05/global-health-rankings/.

[11] Global Footprint Network. n.d. "Country Trends." Accessed January 2, 2024. https://data.footprintnetwork.org/#/countryTrends?cn=67&type=earth.

[12] Konrath, Sara, Edward O'Brien, and Courtney Hsing. 2011. "Changes in Dispositional Empathy in American College Students Over Time: A Meta-Analysis." *Personality and Social Psychology Review,* 15(2): 180 – 198. http://dx.doi.org/10.1177/1088868310377395.

[13] Chopik, William, Deepti Joshi, and Sara H. Konrath. 2014. "Historical changes in American self-interest: State of the Union addresses 1790 to 2012." *Personality and Individual Differences,* 66: 128–133. http://dx.doi.org/10.1016/j.paid.2014.03.015.

[14] Brenan, Megan. 2022. "Americans' Trust in Media

Remains Near Record Low." Gallup, posted October 18, 2022. https://news.gallup.com/poll/403166/americans-trust-media-remains-near-record-low.aspx.

[15] Jones, Jeffery. 2021. "Four in 10 Americans Say They Are Environmentalists." Gallup, posted April 21, 2021. https://news.gallup.com/poll/348227/one-four-americans-say-environmentalists.aspx.

[16] Tyson, Alec, Brian Kennedy, and Cary Funk. 2021. "Gen Z, Millennials Stand Out for Climate Change Activism, Social Media Engagement with Issue." Pew Research Center, posted May 26, 2021. https://www.pewresearch.org/science/2021/05/26/gen-z-millennials-stand-out-for-climate-change-activism-social-media-engagement-with-issue/.

[17] Trahan, Lisa, Karla K. Stuebing, Merril K. Hiscock, and Jack M. Fletcher. 2014. "The Flynn Effect: A Meta-analysis." *Psychol Bull.,* 140(5): 1332–1360. http://dx.doi.org/doi:10.1037/a0037173.

[18] Kucharavy, Dmitry, and Roland De Guio. 2011. "Application of S-shaped curves." *Procedia Engineering,* 9: 559–572. http://dx.doi.org/10.1016/j.proeng.2011.03.142.

[19] Wikipedia. n.d. "Sigmoid function." Accessed February 16, 2024. https://en.wikipedia.org/wiki/Sigmoid_function.

[20] The Daily Show. 2014. "Jon Stewart Tackles the Biden-Trump Rematch That Nobody Wants." YouTube, posted February 13, 2024. https://www.youtube.com/watch?v=NpBPm0b9deQ.

[21] Collins, Ashley. 2018. "A year later: Trump, fake news, white supremacy topics at this year's speak out event." *Naples Daily News,* January 23, 2018. https://eu.naplesnews.com/story/news/local/communities/collier-citizen/2018/01/23/year-later-trump-fake-news-white-supremacy-topics-years-speak-out-

event/1029627001/

22 Stoknes, Per Espen. "How to achieve the Sustainable Development Goals within planetary boundaries by 2050." *Real-World Econ. Rev*, 87 (2019): 230. http://www.paecon.net/PAEReview/issue87/Stoknes87.pdf.

23 Tian, Nan, Diego Lopes Da Silva, Xiao Liang, Lorenzo Scarazzato, Lucie Béraud-Sudreau and Ana Carolina de Oliveira Assis. 2023. "Trends in World Military Expenditure, 2022." Stockholm International Peace Research Institute, posted April 2023. https://www.sipri.org/sites/default/files/2023-04/2304_fs_milex_2022.pdf.

www.ingramcontent.com/pod-product-compliance
Lightning Source LLC
Chambersburg PA
CBHW050910260726
48660CB00001B/132